OPTIMARKETING

Marketing Optimization to Electrify Your Business

ROBERT ROSENTHAL

Two non-marketers who would have loved every word of this.

ACKNOWLEDGEMENTS

I'm lucky – from Day One, I've had spectacular people backing me. Starting with my parents, who loved me unconditionally and conned me into thinking I could accomplish almost anything; brothers Allan, Mark, Eddy, and Larry, who think I'm a lot smarter than I am; relatives and friends in New Jersey, California, New York, Massachusetts, and elsewhere, who've made my life so much richer; Max Lupul, the CSUN professor who cultivated my passion for marketing; pivotal employers Vincent Facciponte, Neal Friedman, Jay Hillis, Henson Lacon, Sandy Files, Ed Nash, Bud Pironti, Jess Joseph, Glenn Shapiro, Vince Amen, Dick Warren, and Bob Russell; the nearly 150 clients we've worked with over a quarter century; talented and passionate writers and artists who evolved the Optimarketing hybrid, including John Sturtevant, Bob Stevenson, David Luhn, Kyrre Carlsen, Bruce Fitzgerald, Michael Russell, Audrey Kerrigan, Diana LoMonaco, and Alex Derrick; the technical and operations experts who've made magic happen and taught me so much, including Bruce Rosenbaum, Craig Cohen, Luke Middleton, and Bilal Asgher; Michael Granoff, the best-ever pitcher of our services; Kelly Yuen, the account director, fixer, and confidante who's gone beyond and above for 13 years; Keith Lane, the creative star who "electrified" this book's subtitle; Sheila Butler, the editor who taught me what excellent writing was really about; my daughter Skyler, who gives her parents more joy than she'll ever know; and my wife Jodi, the great love of my life who kept reminding me to hurry up and get this damn book done.

ABOUT YOUR AUTHOR

Robert Rosenthal believes his North Jersey childhood was the nearly perfect training ground for a marketing career. On the other side of the Hudson River, Robert lived among wonderfully diverse American consumers.

For reasons he doubts he'll ever fully understand, early on, this TV-obsessed baby boomer became convinced he could create better advertising than the then-ubiquitous (and now highly controversial) "Marlboro Man" campaign.

Young Robert couldn't wait to embark on a marketing career and develop better stuff than the guys behind those smoking cowboys. He worked nearly full-time for a marketing firm while attending college full-time as a marketing major.

Robert went on to found Contenteurs, a content marketing agency that has developed record-breaking campaigns for dozens of businesses and won more than 50 awards. He's run thousands of marketing tests; introduced marketers to conceptual direct marketing, creative email advertising, and social media monetization; and conceived Optimarketing.™

Clients have included Bright Horizons, Citigroup, Constant Contact, Eloqua, *Fast Company*, Fidelity Investments, Forrester, Gartner, Harvard, IBM, IDG, *Inc. Magazine*, Infogroup, Iron Mountain, Martha Stewart Living Omnimedia, McGraw-Hill, MIT, Monster, *New England Journal of Medicine*, Progress, RSA, Thomson Reuters, Webby Awards, Ziff Davis, and way too many startups to mention here.

Robert marketed one young business that became America's fastest-growing software firm – and launched another in the U.S. that was ultimately sold for more than $600 million. Total change in value of businesses he's been closely associated with runs in the billions. His agency's work has been covered in *Advertising Age*, *AdWeek*, *Direct Marketing News*, *Target Marketing*, *The New York Times*, among other publications. Robert's also been featured in MarketingSherpa's "Great Minds" series.

He previously held management positions at BBDO Direct, Petersen Publishing, Publishers Choice, and American Management Association. Robert has a Bachelor of Science degree in marketing from California State University, Northridge.

CONTENTS

CONTENTS

"The best way to predict the future is to invent it."
– Alan Kay

INTRODUCTION

Let's start with what this isn't. *Optimarketing: Marketing Optimization to Electrify Your Business* isn't Marketing 101. Nor is it a collection of remarkably easy steps, proprietary secrets, or get-rich-quick schemes. It's definitely not a set of "mysteries revealed." Actually, much of what it covers isn't mysterious at all.

This book is about making the most of what you've got as a marketer. About what it takes to run the best marketing of your career. Even the best in your industry.

Optimarketing: Marketing Optimization to Electrify Your Business is about marketing optimization, pure and simple. Not just one aspect. We're talking across-the-board, whole-enchilada optimization.

To my knowledge, no one has been crazy enough to comprehensively address what it takes to optimize marketing outcomes. Experts tend to discuss only certain aspects of optimization. A writer may cover optimized use of data but omit the power of creative ideas. And although organizational and cultural factors make a huge contribution to outcomes, they generally aren't found on lists of "best practices."

Optimarketing: Marketing Optimization to Electrify Your Business is written for a wide audience – everyone from Presidents to entry-level marketers to Chief Marketing Officers. It's aimed squarely at marketers who execute types of marketing that happen more than 95% of the time. But marketers in ten-figure organizations doing super expensive stuff should find plenty of value here as well. It's designed to teach new tricks to marketers with 20 years under their belt. But it also addresses a set of fundamentals – because they're … well, funda-

1

mentally important contributors to outcomes.

I've always loved a story about John Wooden, legendary UCLA basketball coach. He attracted players like Kareem Abdul-Jabbar – some of the best in America. But after they arrived on the Westwood campus, he showed them how to (get ready for this) properly put on their socks. As well as something basketball players are typically taught in elementary school: how to execute a pick-and-roll. Because Wooden – one of the twentieth century's greatest winners – wanted his team to nail the fundamentals before moving on to other important stuff.

Optimarketing: Marketing Optimization to Electrify Your Business is a series of more than 75 short essays on important marketing topics. Each essay header is written to tip readers off on what we're about to cover. If you think a particular essay isn't up your alley, jump to the next. But I do suggest giving each one a good look. You may find certain things were more important than you initially suspected.

I've read business books that seemed deliberately padded. I vowed not to do that here, and include no more words than necessary. That said, this does indeed cover a considerable amount of ground. But it doesn't do an extremely deep dive into topics deserving their own books (e.g., pay-per-click marketing, copywriting, social media). I didn't want *Optimarketing: Marketing Optimization to Electrify Your Business* to exceed *Infinite Jest* in length. Over time, you may wish to augment this with books focused on one or more topics covered here.

Does this book address every aspect of marketing? Of course not. But if you're out to learn how to break marketing records – and feel more fulfilled in your work – you'll find what you need.

On that note, one should never underestimate the mental side of marketing. Near the end of *Optimarketing: Marketing Optimization to Electrify Your Business*, you'll find a "Mind of the Optimarketer" section you shouldn't miss. I was tempted to place it at the beginning because it's THAT important.

Hopefully some advice you find in these pages will prove timeless. Sprinkled throughout are lessons I picked up from marketing greats. It's always amazed me how few marketers bother learning from Hall of Famers who made their most valuable lessons available for future generations.

I wanted you to know about books that gave me extremely valuable advice. So at the end you'll find a list of those that changed the course of my career.

Now let's see about changing yours.

WHAT IS OPTIMARKETING?

Optimarketing is a marketing optimization methodology our marketing agency evolved over 25 years after running thousands of tests and keeping score the entire time.

It's about optimizing all major contributors to marketing outcomes. Among other things, Optimarketing unites unconventional creative thinking with sophisticated measurable marketing techniques. A fitting metaphor (please forgive me but it works): It's like firing on all pistons.

Optimarketing also builds on more than 100 years of measurable marketing history. It encompasses not just commonly scrutinized elements like creative, media, and offers, but other important factors like test quality, mathematical soundness, and corporate culture.

Scattered throughout this book you'll find the term "Optimarketer." Optimarketers make every effort to optimize all major marketing elements. They're some of the most valuable players in marketing.

CASE EXAMPLE: IRON MOUNTAIN

Here's a good illustration of what could happen when a marketer optimizes all major elements. Prior to working with our marketing agency, Iron Mountain, the data storage and records management giant, averaged a .4% response rate on direct mail for one of its services. We moved the needle all the way up to 4% – a tenfold increase. What did we do differently? Get ready for an important lesson: Our team changed just about everything. We added a compelling creative concept, new offer, different format, easier feedback collection, and more productive mailing lists. If you're out to transform marketing outcomes, you want to manipulate as many important elements as possible.

DISCARD YESTERDAY'S MARKETING PLAYBOOK

Hear about the white-hot brand recently launched using only blockbuster television commercials?

I know – you didn't. Because the brand doesn't exist.

At one time, television advertising was capable of creating megabrands. But today you wouldn't find a competent marketer walking the earth who'd rely on TV only. At a minimum, that launch would include a pronounced digital component.

The marketer who saw 2% direct mail response rates at the end of the 20th century would most likely see a rate south of 1% today. Batch-and-blast email? It's tanked to a similar degree. Even that web landing page that converted more than 50% of visitors 10 years ago would probably convert a substantially lower percentage right now.

What marketers have traditionally pushed no longer pulls.

Reasons are well-known: Many prospects no longer accept conventional sales pitches. Consumers don't just have more power; they have more options. As a marketer, you're either a provider of value or you're irrelevant.

Now for the good news: Human nature hasn't changed. The word "free" resonates as much as ever. And techniques taught to marketers for decades – like idea-building, storytelling, and testing – remain hugely important.

It's time to toss yesterday's playbook and work from one that delivers what today's skeptical, busy, discriminating customers want – as intelligently, efficiently, and imaginatively as possible.

Now let's talk about making it happen.

LEARN THE RULES –
THEN GROW BEYOND THEM

From the moment we're spanked on the ass as newborns, we're exposed to rules. Marketers deal with them constantly. Today they're often called "best practices." Many have glaring shortcomings. Some no longer apply.

Let's discuss David Ogilvy – an advertising legend. I learned a lot from his books. To this day, I apply what he taught me.

But the Ogilvy & Mather co-founder wrote *Confessions of an Advertising Man* in 1963 – the "Mad Men" era. In it, he famously said "People don't buy from clowns." After reading that, generations of advertising pros refused to run humorous ads that could have been more profitable than what they went with. He also claimed reverse type was ALWAYS deadly. (Ogilvy was right about reverse type when used with long copy. But in short headlines? Come on.)

Clearly, it's best not to treat the precepts of Ogilvy, or any old masters who left the scene long ago, as gospel.

Study Picasso's early work and you'll notice he was a classically trained artist. He mastered the academic rules of his craft. But as a young man, Picasso broke with many of his contemporaries and began creating groundbreaking art. Today, when admirers speak of Picasso's body of work, they break it down by innovation period (e.g., Cubism, Rose, Blue).

Optimarketers selectively choose when to apply the old rules, and often build on them. They don't simply run with a "5-step plan for success." Nor do they

8

operate from a marketing "cookbook" or take a "paint-by-numbers" approach. They defy convention.

They're revolutionaries – wearing smiles. They know how to work the system – and work with people. They get things done. They're able to innovate inside organizations not previously known for innovation. And they're not a tribute band honoring dead marketing legends. They operate in the here and now.

And speaking of rules…

THE "40/40/20 RULE" IS HISTORY

As a young guy in the business, I was a proud member of the direct marketing orthodoxy. Direct marketing fundamentalists are devout: They believe in rules. One of the most famous: the 40/40/20 Rule. It states that 40% of a direct marketing outcome is due to media; 40% is due to the offer; and only 20% is due to creative. Of course, at the time this rule was conceived, few direct marketers were doing interesting creative. So it was no surprise direct marketing creative rarely lifted outcomes by big margins.

But today, talented people create work that qualifies as direct marketing. Technology gives us an ability to deeply understand which messaging directions are most likely to succeed. And it's never been easier to measure the contribution of creative.

In controlled testing, we've seen response-rate increases in excess of 100% entirely by virtue of creative. This doesn't mean that media and offer aren't essential. They are. But claiming that the creative element impacts only 20% of the outcome in all cases is simply false.

RESEARCH: YOUR CONSISTENT OUTCOME-RAISER

Most marketing campaigns aren't research-based or based on valid research. Far more should be for a simple reason: Outcomes are better when marketing is backed by reliable – and of course, highly useful – research on the front end.

Doesn't matter if you have an IQ approaching that of Marilyn vos Savant (who evidently beat Einstein's score): In marketing, you're largely as good as your information. Research isn't just important; it's often make-or-break stuff.

Marketers have long relied upon research data. Before opening his own agency, the famous ad guy I mentioned a moment ago, David Ogilvy, worked for George Gallup, where he developed a passion for leveraging research data in advertising. It stayed with him throughout his spectacular career and gave his agency a competitive edge.

Back in Ogilvy's day, and over several subsequent decades, primary research (collecting data that doesn't yet exist) was often a fairly expensive proposition. Statistically projectable mail and telephone surveys weren't cheap. Focus groups – those artificial get-togethers of moderators sitting with "prospects" listening to each others' responses while client and agency observe via a one-way mirror while munching on sandwiches – weren't just costly, but often unreliable.

Since then, we've seen several major marketing research innovations. In the 1980s, account planning became popular in some major agencies. Account

11

planners don't just listen to consumers; they spend serious time with them in their own environments. As a result, creative work that emerges from account planning is often more genuine, compelling, and responsive. It's an approach worth serious consideration.

As are web-based surveys. Typically they aren't as in-depth as one-on-one interviews, but they're capable of yielding valuable insights. Many feature-rich survey tools are free (or almost free) and provide marketers with hierarchal and other helpful data.

Thinking of producing an educational video series and want to defy convention by learning which unconventional topics will be most popular? Deploy a web-based survey to your prospects and you may get an accurate ranking of priorities in minutes. And if you find an imaginative way to encourage people to respond, the response rate could be exceptional. In fact, if the incentive is strong enough, a web-based research study could also be a lead generator.

But what if you'd rather not do your own research? In many cases, recent, relevant research done by others (secondary research) is far better than nothing.

Whatever you do, don't simply rely on someone like your mother-in-law, even if you think she's in the target group. There's a good chance you'll be led astray.

Don't "run it up the flagpole" by simply going from cubicle to cubicle and taking a tally instead of banking on valid research. Early in my career, I grimaced when colleagues "led the witness" by placing an ad in front of a co-worker and suggesting "Don't you think people will see this and say to themselves…"

Research from inside one's office tends to be fatally flawed. Co-workers aren't your target group. The sample size is usually inadequate. The manner of presenting options may be biased. And you may receive feedback that's about another agenda rather than the information you're seeking.

Now let's talk about the most accurate research of all. As the web took off as an advertising medium, the popularity of live testing (e.g., split-run tests of different options in Google AdWords) grew exponentially. Rather then rely on what consumers *say* they'll buy, with live testing, marketers see what they actually buy in the real world. When they make sense, live tests run in projectable ways are superior to other forms of research, including focus groups.

One word of caution: Never do research merely for the sake of … doing research. Set it up so findings are, for lack of a better word, actionable.

COLLABORATION BEATS COMMAND AND CONTROL

After college, when I marched (pun intended) into the full-time work world, a large share of executives were World War II vets. Much of what they knew about management was acquired while serving their country.

In the military, soldiers are taught to follow orders and not question them. It's a command-and-control structure. I didn't serve, so I can't speak with expertise about armed services protocol. But I do know something about business and marketing in particular. In marketing, we need productive collaboration – not command and control.

Have you noticed each new generation of marketers has less tolerance for authoritarian regimes? I recall an autocratic company president who, when given details on a collaborative process that brought together the best thinking inside and outside his company, smirked and said *he* was the only one needing to be consulted. Businesses take a financial hit when executives make ego-driven decisions like that.

Marketers at all levels should feel comfortable questioning anything and everything at any time. Each year I attend meetings with marketers apparently afraid to disagree with the boss. Show me a marketing group where employees march in lockstep and I'll show you one making costly (and unnecessary) mistakes.

Some of the most energizing meetings I've been in were those where an observer would have had a hard time distinguishing between internal and external people – or between the boss and everyone else.

Great ideas can – and do – come from everywhere. But when workers are worried about how their ideas will be received, they're less likely to speak up. A great way to raise outcomes is to ensure everyone feels free to be heard. It's often best to have the highest-paid person speak last, to encourage more (and more unbiased) contributions.

In a business world increasingly more interdependent, it's vital to nurture relationships with external contributors. Optimarketers welcome people from the outside who bring valuable skills to the table. Unfortunately, some marketers feel threatened and try competing with these experts. Or even attempt to undermine their success altogether.

Marketers who operate this way may feel insecure about their role and get pressure from their boss to have a tight-knit group do all important thinking.

Your outcomes will be better if you and your colleagues support outside contributors. To make this consistently happen, employee performance evaluations should cover relationships with partners. Employees should be rewarded for maintaining strong relationships inside and outside the company.

How you collaborate makes a serious bottom-line difference.

A BUSINESS OF IDEAS

Here's something at the Category 5 level for anyone aiming for excellence: Marketing is, above all, a business of ideas. Fascinating, relevant, smart, responsive, and, yes, kickass ideas.

Thanks to the great equalizer, the Internet, it's now easier for smaller businesses to whup exponentially larger (and often more ossified) businesses by embracing superior marketing ideas.

But for this to happen, you can't keep your head buried in tools and reports. You've got to enter the realm of great big ideas.

The good news: That realm doesn't necessarily require great big budgets. While it's true that marketing innovation requires a budget, the best ideas are often relatively cheap to pull off. And they may even make a tiny budget look huge.

George Parker, hilarious AdScam blogger and brilliant adman, said great advertising requires money, information, and time. All absolutely true. And I'm sure George would agree that the quality of people doing the actual work is a huge contributor to outcomes. Hire George Parker as your copywriter and you'll have much better odds of success than if you hire George Blow (Joe's cousin).

It's like baseball: Players most likely to hit it out of the park are those who've belted home runs most often in the past. *Who* does the work often matters more than *what* work gets done.

Highly accomplished teams know that greatness rarely happens by accident:

16

It usually results from a deliberate process. We call it "controlled chaos" (emphasis on the latter term). In fact, introduce too much process in creative endeavors and you may end up empty-handed. DDB co-founder Bill Bernbach said, "Logic and over-analysis can immobilize and sterilize an idea. It's like love – the more you analyze it the faster it disappears." Don't put that idea under a microscope.

So let's talk about how to create marketing amazingness. It's not simply about how smart you are – innovation is a team sport. A collaborative enterprise.

We've found it best to kick off collaborations by sending the client written questions, so "subject matter experts" know exactly what we need to innovate.

Early on, we become scholars of their marketing history. Of course, we also study up on the competition and review recent research.

But to innovate, you can't just stare at documents. You've got to have conversations with the right people at the right times. So on the front end, we do our own set of one-on-one interviews. A colleague once called these "emotion mining."

From there, we often collect hundreds (repeat, *hundreds*) of ideas in order to run just one. We shake things up by reframing the problem or challenge, asking new questions, or thinking in opposites.

An unwritten rule: Never stop at the first idea. Go for idea quantity and save the critical evaluation for later. During the collection phase, there are no "bad" ideas, whereas building on those conceived by others is encouraged.

All this relates to what's commonly known as brainstorming. Advertising people tend to be proponents of group brainstorming. These sessions are indeed useful. But we've found it important also to engage in solidary idea-building. A recent study indicated that individual brainstorming tends to be even more productive than group brainstorming. Recommendation: Do both.

Whether you're on your own or in a group, you must empty your brain of the typical and expected until you arrive at exceptional stuff. The process should feel organic, loose, exciting, and fun – not forced. When things are really humming, it may seem as if ideas are falling from the sky.

While collecting ideas, mix up your environment. Don't sit in the same spot all day and night. Get in the car and go for a ride. Or hop on a train.

Learn what time of day works best for you to grow ideas. Mick Jagger said his songwriting skills are sharpest in the early morning. I'm no Rolling Stone, but I often come up with the most exciting ideas before 11 a.m. Through experimentation, discover what time of day works best for you.

After you arrive at a collection of ideas that feel sufficiently great, pass them through a filter. Do they have to be campaignable? Implementable within a particular timeframe or a budget that doesn't exceed X dollars?

Leave behind work you consider derivative, boring, not smart, a stretch, or trite. If your gut tells you it's been done to death, and you've been unable to add a new dimension, go with your gut and move on.

Naturally, what gets presented varies widely from case to case, but it's a good idea to explore – and share – emotional and psychological directions, including those that make the customer the hero (a departure from my early days in marketing, when pundits recommended making the product the hero).

Watch out for colleagues who act all-knowing. As a young agency guy, I heard account people proclaim, "The client will *never* okay that."

Just think about that comment. How could anyone make an accurate call in advance about what a client would "never" approve after seeing a top-notch presentation and understanding the rationale behind it? While growing ideas, never censor yourself by trying to read the client's mind. Give them more credit; treat them like grownups. Share everything you consider interesting.

When I was starting out, an older guy recommended showing the client a few ideas they expected and one I loved. I quickly realized that many marketers approve the concept they expected. That's why it's best to leave mediocrity off the table. Share only ideas you consider potentially great. Because if you present ordinary work, not only might it be accepted – there's an excellent chance it *will* be accepted.

Funny thing about groundbreaking ideas – they often scare the shit out of people. It's usually easier to approve what's considered safe, familiar, and devoid of risk. Executives who aren't experienced with outstanding concepts often get behind pedestrian work – even vanilla ideas out of left field – simply to stay within their comfort zone.

Some managers lack the skill to identify exceptional concepts. In these cases, it's best for them to defer to others. One's past experience (or lack thereof) shouldn't limit a marketing team's future potential.

Optimarketers are out to run ideas that make a big difference. To borrow from a description of DDB's legendary Volkswagen campaign during advertising's Creative Revolution, that means "zagging while others zig." But it doesn't mean edgy ideas are always best. Don't do edgy strictly for the sake of edgy.

Remember, we're doing something hard: changing behavior. One powerful way of doing this is to change habits. In *The Power of Habit*, author Charles Duhigg shares the story of how it became common for consumers to brush their teeth at least twice a day. Basically, an advertising campaign convinced them to do it. It's been that way ever since. Change habits and you've done something extraordinary as a marketer.

Despite all the talk, many teams – including those with no shortage of swagger – consistently produce ordinary work. One common reason: a "Not Made Here" attitude keeps pushing them to accept only what's created internally. Again, this shortcoming often stems from insecurity. It's costly, because diverse problem-solving teams enjoy a better rate of success.

Want to solve a marketing problem? Don't just invite marketers to sit at the table. Bring together people with a range of perspectives.

Then there's the false belief that it's inappropriate to run novel marketing in a seemingly special or unique industry (but appropriate to bore prospects with undifferentiated work). We've successfully introduced novel ideas in a full range of situations – including companies selling seven- and eight-figure relationships.

There's simply no excuse to run me-too, mind-numbing marketing. I've yet to find an industry that couldn't benefit from excellent conceptual work and outstanding ideas. Don't be limited by the shortcomings, biases, or fears of colleagues – including those in a position to make the call.

On that note, some marketers leave decisions about creative ideas to the highest paid person, who may not be most likely to make the best call.

Then we have self-styled "devil's advocates." Remember, almost anyone can tear down an idea in its infancy. It's surprisingly easy. But builders of ideas are far more valuable than critics.

Remember, if an awesome idea gets killed, you don't get points for coming up with it. As the saying goes, "If it didn't run, it never happened." So make it happen.

And do respect the all-important execution phase. A valuable concept development tip we picked up from Luke Sullivan in *Hey Whipple, Squeeze This*: It's best to leave ample time to sculpt what may be a diamond in the rough. And to give the team that creates that excellent idea room to finish what they conceived. When building ideas – and campaigns – much of the most important work happens at the tail end.

From a conceptual standpoint, you could say we're in the midst of a crisis. Few campaigns are exceptional. It's a wide open opportunity for ambitious marketers. Take advantage of it.

CASE EXAMPLE: THE *NEW ENGLAND JOURNAL OF MEDICINE*

The *New England Journal of Medicine* is written, of course, for physicians. Like many publishers of professional journals, NEJM relies on email marketing to attract subscribers. Our job was to beat a control email marketing approach. The control ad (which we were asked to improve upon) prominently featured a free issue offer. The offer was the big driver; the ad didn't include a concept. Our test ad contained a prehead with the control offer and the headline "What reading it says about you." Below that headline three callouts next to a photo of a physician read "Maintains the highest standards," "Committed to remaining current," and "Passionate about medicine." In the body copy, the story fleshed out what reading NEJM says about physicians. And we went toe-to-toe with the control approach on the free issue offer. So our test ad represented the best of both worlds: a strongly merchandised offer plus an emotional and relevant concept. Result: Our test ad pulled in 97% more revenue than the control ad did.

WHY DON'T BIG BUSINESSES RUN BIG IDEAS MORE OFTEN?

Some businesses have 100 times the marketing budget of their competitors. So they're about 100 times more likely to run innovative marketing, right? Nope.

With far more resources than smaller businesses, you'd expect larger ones to do great things far more often. But marketing innovation tends to happen more frequently in smaller organizations, for several reasons.

Bigger businesses tend to accumulate more procedures, processes, guidelines, and rules. Many are in place for good reasons, but some aren't and just gum things up. Larger entities are often more risk-averse than competitors with less to lose and more fire in the corporate belly.

Extra-large entities generally have more hierarchy and thus more barriers to innovation. They form committees more often. There's an old saying that goes something like this: "Visit any park and you'll never find a monument dedicated to a committee." Committees often green-light ordinary marketing and rarely approve anything extraordinary.

So, what can bigger businesses do to get big ideas to run more often? Remove barriers to innovation. Support a culture of experimentation. Give managers more decision-making authority. Keep the team focused on the right agenda. Benefit from diversity by bringing in more groundbreaking marketers – especially those with an entrepreneurial spirit – and giving them what they need to do their best work.

WHAT GREAT MARKETING CAMPAIGNS HAVE IN COMMON

When marketers talk about campaign consistency, they often dwell on graphics. In many cases, consistent graphics do a good job connecting campaign executions in consumers' minds. But that's the relatively easy part.

Let's say your campaign's goals are to achieve a particular revenue figure – while winning hearts and minds.

Your product has a set of benefits. Differentiators. Problems it solves. We know the best ads in any media tend to be focused. And the best advertisers are often great storytellers.

What does all this mean? Every campaign execution is a chance to reveal another essential facet of your story. The cumulative effect: You chisel away at prospects' objections. Stay top-of-mind. And win them over.

Your audience should be treated to a consistent experience as they move from email ad to landing page to web video to Facebook post. But a campaign's connective tissue takes a variety of forms. It doesn't require a consistent tagline or mascot. It certainly doesn't require components that look virtually identical.

Think back over the Nike ads you've seen for decades. They've often been wildly different. But what's remained consistent has been Nike's mission, values, beliefs, voice, and attitude.

24

The very best campaigns clarify. Amplify. Differentiate. Move consumers to act. And earn outstanding profits. You'll find lots of ways to make it all happen.

Most creators of marketing campaigns don't aim high enough. Few marketers are driving campaigns that could be categorized as spectacular. It's a huge opportunity for ambitious marketers.

As Teddy Roosevelt famously said, "Dare to be great."

LAUNCH A CAMPAIGN – OR A MOVEMENT

Guy Kawasaki, Apple's former Chief Evangelist and one of the planet's great marketing leaders, said (I'm paraphrasing): "Don't start a campaign; launch a movement."

Movements tend to accomplish more than campaigns. Often way more. Think back to the 2008 U.S. presidential election. John McCain ran a campaign; backers of Barack Obama drove a movement. We all know what happened there.

A campaign is about a product, service, company – or all three. A movement is about something greater. People forge emotional connections with movements. They invest in them.

But business managers can't just wake up and say "Let's launch a movement." You see, any business can run a campaign; few can legitimately lead a movement. The overwhelming majority of businesses aren't a movement and never will be.

This can't be faked. When a business becomes a movement, it tends to be driven more by consumers than the marketer.

THE VALUE OF POSITIONING – AND REPOSITIONING

In *Positioning: The Battle for Your Mind*, Al Ries and Jack Trout talk about the limited slots consumers have in their brain for products and services, and the importance of "positioning" one's business in the ideal slot. Or even placing your business in a "category of one."

They also discuss *repositioning* – changing the position a business occupies in consumers' minds. Something I've long found fascinating: Repositioning one's competition. It's not easy. And rarely done. But marketers who pull it off are, in my view, operating at the top of their game.

A close-to-home example: When I was a kid, we always had peanut butter in the house. Besides peanut butter and jelly sandwiches, we regularly ate peanut butter and Marshmallow Fluff sandwiches. My recommendation: Avoid the fluff (happens to be a good metaphor). PBJ is much easier to digest and healthier.

But I digress. Back to my childhood. The big three brands were Skippy, Peter Pan, and Jif. One day, Jif began running ads with the tagline "Choosey moms choose Jif." Suddenly, Jif's competitors were repositioned as products for mothers who didn't give a damn about the food their kids consumed. What mother didn't want to think of herself as a "choosey" mom?

The Jif brand succeeded at making mothers feel like lousy parents for buying peanut butter other than Jif. Repositioning is beyond powerful.

CASE EXAMPLE: NORDSON EFD

Nordson EFD makes automated fluid dispensers costing hundreds of dollars per unit – and worth every penny. They're used when manufacturers need to apply consistent glue dots and don't have room for error. At the time of a product-line launch, alternatives to EFD fluid dispensers were perceived as free or dirt cheap. They included squeeze bottles and even toothpicks. We repositioned these inferior substitutes as ultimately far more expensive and possibly even dangerous. In one ad we displayed a box of toothpicks (which, of course, would sell for next to nothing) with a sign reading "Fluid Applicators – $1,682/Box." The headline referred to "The real cost of manual fluid dispensers." Opening body copy read "Talk about penny wise and pound foolish! Add the cost of product rejects, rework and returns, plus fluid waste, and you'll probably conclude the 'almost free' stuff you're using to apply assembly fluids is costing you a bloody fortune." Result: According to EFD's head of marketing, this campaign for a new product line was the company's most profitable launch ever.

SWEET EMOTION (HT AEROSMITH)

As a college marketing major, my professors drilled into me that studies for decades indicated that emotional and psychological concepts often resonate far more than feature-and-function ones. Think of how many purchases you've made over the years that were largely driven by emotion.

Looking back over the record-breaking campaigns we've run, many of the strongest were indeed cases where we successfully used psychology. Features certainly have their place – but it's often best to place them underneath an emotional concept.

It's been said that a great campaign can transform a business – or even launch a business category. Emotional concepts have that potential.

WHAT WE LEARNED ABOUT FINDING THE OPTIMAL BALANCE

In our marketing agency's early days, we operated straight from the classic direct marketing playbook. Then we began experimenting with concepts typically associated with creatively focused shops.

At first we ran conceptually strong advertising – with the concept cranked at full blast – but played down the offer, to amp up the creative. The response rate dropped in controlled testing against more offer-centric advertising. So we made adjustments.

The big finding: When we optimized the presentation of both concept and offer, we beat even the strongest conventional direct marketing. By nailing the art and science sides of our work, we were running, in measurable terms, our most successful marketing.

The timing was good: Many marketers no longer had a separate line item for brand-building and direct marketing. The work had to do both. And it did.

How did we optimize the concept *and* offer? When offering a product demo, we pushed it hard, right from the get-go. So in that sense, we went toe-to-toe with the direct marketing orthodoxy. But we overlaid an excellent conceptual piece. So we captured the imagination of viewers while waving an enticing carrot.

For decades, marketers had the choice between interesting conceptual work and strong response marketing. Essentially, they were asked to pick one. Opti-marketing is about doing both.

COPYWRITING TO MAKE EVERY WORD COUNT

"The real giants have always been poets, men who jumped from facts into the realm of imagination and ideas." – Bill Bernbach

Having written and directed the creation of well over 1,000 ads in various media (almost all of which were tracked), I've learned some things about the word side of marketing. Many of the greatest copywriting lessons come from old masters. I'll share some of them here, along with my own thoughts.

Let's start with some things top copywriters know and a large number of marketers routinely overlook: Specifics tend to outsell generalizations. Facts outsell empty claims. And benefits outsell features.

Samuel Johnson said "Promise, large promise, is the soul of an advertisement." Johnson was mostly right. It's hard to go wrong by appealing to self-interest.

I recall a story I heard early in my career but never forgot. When the contents of the Anchor Brewery were being auctioned off, the auctioneer said, "We are not here to sell boilers and vats, but the potentiality of growing rich beyond the dreams of avarice."

Yet it's important to balance thinking like that with something found in the old Kenyon & Eckhardt *Book of Creative Standards.* They said the promise in an ad is like a balloon: Blow it up too much and it bursts. According to K & E:

"A breath of truth, blown up to improbable size, gets stretched beyond all believabil-

ity. So no one (except the advertiser) takes it seriously. Customers avert their minds from the inflated claim, the big boast headline, the unparalleled superlative."

We've all seen ads so incredible they weren't credible. Very often, the strongest ads are understated. Superlative-free.

Sometimes an excellent move is to reveal your imperfections. One of the most famous ads ever, for Volkswagen, contained a one-word headline: "Lemon." Opening body copy below a VW photo read, "This Volkswagen missed the boat. The chrome strip on the glove compartment is blemished and must be replaced. Chances are, you wouldn't have noticed it; Inspector Kurt Kroner did." Copy went on to talk about a "preoccupation with detail." The "Lemon" ad became a textbook example of how to optimize credibility.

So pull back on adjectives. And especially exclamation points. Substantiate your claims. Don't bother using testimonials signed "Barbara P.," or curiously round statistical boasts like "I achieved a 100% increase!" Even if they're real, people won't believe you. State the truth with verisimilitude – the appearance of truth.

The best copywriters are outstanding storytellers. They write person-to-person and come off as human beings, not businesses. They avoid clichés, analyst-speak, and unnecessary buzzwords. As a result, they draw more people in – and get more of them to act.

These writers craft presentations that run in logical order. They nail the hierarchy of copy points. Their advertising is beautifully choreographed.

Another master of the word business, Victor Schwab, said an ad should take the reader from where he is to where you want him to be. From headline to call-to-action, everything is meticulously thought through. It flows almost poetically. Optimarketers make copy sing. (Thank you, Ed Nash, for teaching me that.)

I like the comparison of lightning vs. lightning bug to describe the difference between the perfect word and a merely serviceable one. You should make every word count.

When writing, be imaginative – but don't force readers to use their imagination. Remember this maxim: Think it out square, say it with flair. Caveat: What you say will generally be more important than how you say it.

Don't dumb down your copy. Treat your reader intelligently. David Ogilvy famously said "The consumer is not a moron; she is your wife." But never inject language that creates ambiguity or causes confusion.

And what about headlines? Yeah, they're hugely important – and misunderstood. The goal of the headline isn't to merely "capture attention." Anyone can throw a four-letter word into a headline and accomplish that. No, the actual goal is to get as many of the right readers as possible to start the ad in the right frame of mind.

It's true, a benefit-oriented headline often works. But not always. People who craft great advertising headlines know there are lots of ways to bring readers into an ad.

Edit the hell out of your copy. When you think it's all set, print it out and read it aloud, dramatically. Fix the bumps, and then repeat. If you need 24 drafts to get it where you want it, go through two dozen drafts.

Address your audience appropriately, all things considered, but be contemporary. As Bill Bernbach said, "Speak in today's idiom."

Here's an example of the difference a few words can make: I once changed three words in a headline to promote a book for woodworkers on making animated toys. Just three words. In split-run testing, orders rose from 337 to 412, and profits leaped from 34% to 63% – an 85% increase.

Optimarketers have the skill and guts to break new ground in advertising copy – while incorporating at least some of the fundamentals found here.

If you're interested in copywriting, I encourage you to learn from masters who shared their greatest lessons in beautifully written books. Writers like Claude Hopkins, John Caples, Maxwell Sackheim, David Ogilvy, Herschell Gordon Lewis, and Robert Bly will give you timeless tips. In the older books, some content will be dated, but much of it will be invaluable.

Here's a tip from one of those guys that has served me well: "New" is either the best or second best word in marketing.

DOES GRAPHIC DESIGN STILL MATTER? HELL, YEAH

My younger brothers call me "Word Man." That gives you an idea of my graphic design ability. But I've learned from spectacular designers.

In this build-your-own-marketing era, it's easy to discount the importance of high-quality graphic design. Just about anyone can log into an ad builder, comb through a stock photography site, and create "visual" advertising. The process tends to be quick, cheap, and easy. But it rarely results in extraordinary work.

Superior graphic design respects the viewer's intelligence. It's smart instead of trite. Surprising instead of expected. Imaginative instead of mundane.

It doesn't spoon-feed the audience. It allows the reader to discover and, yes, to think (but not work too hard). It raises credibility while building trust. It makes a brand more deserving of their attention – and money. It cements emotional connections. It engages.

It's also *au courant*. While our agency was evolving the Optimarketing hybrid, Richard Kirshenbaum, co-founder of Kirshenbaum Bond + Partners and co-author of *Under the Radar*, advised us to pay close attention to what's happening in areas like fashion, because they remain at the cutting edge of design. Richard suggested we have a *Vogue* subscription delivered to our office, to elevate our work in categories like software.

Today it's not terribly difficult for graphic design to be the source of a competitive edge.

Brands have invested in art direction and graphic design for decades for a simple reason: It pays. Had it not been worthwhile, the most sophisticated business executives would have put the money elsewhere.

Bottom line: When the stakes are significant, invest in quality graphic design. Because it's good for your brand – and your bottom line.

BRANDING – WITHOUT THE B.S.

A brand is indeed a promise – and more.

Brands reduce or even eliminate perceived risk. They put to rest doubts about startups and other small businesses. They make life easier for consumers.

When I buy Oreos ("Milk's Favorite Cookie"), I don't worry for a second about being disappointed. I expect product quality to be great, regardless of where I pick up a package. The Oreos brand has yet to let me down.

When my daughter buys TOMS shoes, she feels fashionable *and* pleased with herself because of the company's "buy a pair, give a pair" approach.

Great brands aren't seen just as safe. They create a set of positive associations in the heads of consumers that often make a profound bottom-line difference over time.

Every touch point is part of the consumer's brand experience. It's much more than marketing. It's product, people, service, guarantee, customers, stores, offices, values, culture, and more.

Branding is everyone's job. That's why it's a little silly for a design agency to talk about launching a "branding initiative."

Many of these efforts were previously known as "corporate identity programs" (often a fancy term for corporate graphics systems). Apparently, one day someone at an agency realized "branding initiatives" earned higher fees.

Don't get me wrong – agencies often contribute significantly to brand image. A great agency will dig deep to create a campaign reflecting the soul of a business. Many shops talk about brand DNA; in a way, the best ones sorta get to that level. They bring out the underlying greatness of a business.

And branding isn't the province of a particular type of marketing team. A former boss, Ed Nash, founder of BBDO Direct and author of *Direct Marketing: Strategy, Planning, Execution,* said advertising in all media – including direct response – has an awareness byproduct. It's all potentially brand-building.

Many marketers don't realize their potential because they fail to sufficiently stretch the brand. They stay inside what they believe are safe limits and avoid taking risks that could pay off big. Too often, managers deem an important innovation "not brand appropriate" for no good reason. Optimarketers help brands stretch appropriately.

Using pop culture, I'll share an example of a brand that successfully stretched. Justin Timberlake is a singer. He's also a brand. Besides music, he appears in film and even dabbles in comedy – including fairly edgy comedy (see "Dick In a Box"). By appropriately stretching his brand, Justin enhances his appeal as a musical artist.

When anything inhibits innovation – including a creative brief or book of brand guidelines – it's time to change things. Never be slavishly devoted to anything that locks out your ability to produce amazing work.

But do devote yourself to teamwork. True brand building results from cross-functional and cross-disciplinary collaboration. Art directors sit with copywriters, social media experts, film directors, publicists – you name it.

It's a team sport.

DON'T JUST IMITATE. ORIGINATE

Our work has been ripped off again and again. In fact, a major marketing figure did it fairly recently.

Marketers (particularly direct marketers) write about "borrowing" ideas: the practice of running ideas created by others. Many direct marketers proudly keep what's known as a "swipe file."

To many outside direct marketing, I imagine this seems wrong. And in a percentage of cases it absolutely is, for a variety of reasons. But it's also accurate to say very few marketing programs are 100% original.

Concepts that hold out the possibility of greater wealth or popularity or quality of life aren't new. Nor are offers of free trials or white papers or premiums.

In a way, advertisements are like movies: When you get down to it, there are a modest number of themes. Among the most common: fear and greed.

As for content, headlines tend to include a benefit. Art is often integrated, as is a compelling offer and call to action. All this is based on fundamentals evolved through trial and error by others over decades. So in a way, we're all standing on the shoulders of our predecessors.

But blatant creative rip-offs are another matter. They signal to prospects and customers that the advertiser has nothing new to contribute. In the age of social media, there's the added risk of being publicly outed as a rip-off artist.

40

The amount of marketing that looks and sounds very similar is a real problem. It seems many marketers don't set their sights high enough, and push toward the lowest common denominator. Enlightened marketers who study results know mediocre creative work is a prescription for mediocre outcomes.

TIMING IS (ALMOST) EVERYTHING

Optimarketers have exceptional characteristics – including impeccable timing. Besides being good at personal time management, marketers on top of their game keep the timing of marketing programs as close to ideal as possible.

When an extraordinary event happens (e.g., favorable report by the American Medical Association becomes a *New York Times* feature story), they capitalize on it with related marketing – hours or even minutes after the news breaks. And, of course, they respond similarly to negative coverage.

Great marketers make excellent use of time in a variety of other ways. They know leads begin decreasing in value within moments of arrival – so they use autorespond to remain as timely as possible. Nurture and cross-sell programs happen at ideal intervals. Timely marketing programs are triggered by other events (e.g., abandoned shopping cart, time to replenish, or even birthdays).

In many cases, it's about staying in touch in relevant and useful ways at an interval that enables you to be there when circumstances change – including the emergence of a "pain point."

SIMPLIFY

In marketing, more is often less. Less compelling. Less efficient. Less profitable.

Ads, videos, proposals, reports, plans – work you produce should include no more than necessary. As I said earlier, every word should count. (Hmm, could that have been shorter?)

The disease of excessiveness is by no means confined to the creative side. Early in my career, I interacted with a marketing consultant who developed kludgy media plans so complex, no one but she could understand them. Eventually I realized her outcomes were no better than average, but she had managed to lock in her position by making it appear as if she were irreplaceable.

If you attended college, I imagine at least one professor presented the acronyn K.I.S.S. (keep it simple, stupid). When I originally heard that as a college student, I considered it harsh. But today I appreciate its importance.

Optimarketers remove pointless complexity. But that doesn't mean they take the flavor out of headlines or other copy. They look for the best solution, all things considered. They relentlessly search for ways to replace three words with one and improve the sentence. Or eliminate an entire paragraph that adds zero value.

When doing marketing planning, Optimarketers eliminate all unnecessary elements. Speaking of which, much of marketing planning comes down to where you are, where you want to be, and how you're going to get there. (Thank you, Ed Nash, for teaching me that as well.) Simpler marketing plans and go-to-market strategies are easier to articulate, understand, approve, and implement.

Simplification is about dropping the dog-and-pony show and focusing on genuine optimization. It may even free up time for transformation.

We see the benefits of simplification across the marketing spectrum. Users of marketing automation often find it more profitable to introduce what we call "easily consumable content." These meaningful moments impact lead scoring, the number of leads routed to sales, and even conversions.

TEMPLATE FAIL

These days, a lot of marketers must do more with less. In some cases, much more. So they rely on different tools to make it happen. That's where marketing templates come in.

Templates are particularly common in online marketing, including email. When they help marketers win more customers at a highly efficient rate, they're clearly a good thing. But in certain cases they handcuff marketers and inhibit innovation.

Marketers should be free to properly showcase concepts, merchandise offers, and tell stories. Contrary to what some marketers believe, stock photography often isn't the best answer. In fact, it's a leading contributor to work that appears perfectly ordinary – and produces ordinary outcomes.

When a template interferes with success, it's time to get a new template – or work without one. Advertising that looks common is less responsive. Remember, it pays to invest in quality graphic design.

In one case, for a major B2B marketer, we tested fresh, high-quality graphic design in email marketing against the firm's template and lifted clickthroughs by 41%. (At the time, the client was unable to track beyond clickthroughs.)

Visionary marketer Eliot Frick pointed me to this Marshal McLuhan quote: "We shape our tools, and thereafter our tools shape us." Don't let your tools turn you into a garden-variety marketer.

OFFER OPTIMIZATION IS LIKE THAT FACEBOOK STATUS UPDATE (IT'S COMPLICATED)

Let's start with a common question: What exactly is this thing called an "offer?" The offer is what you ask prospects or customers to accept. It's the bait and/or terms that create leads, trials, orders, members, subscribers, or buyers. The offer could be anything from a free product demonstration to a simple invitation to buy something for $29.99.

As contributors to outcomes go, the offer ain't everything, but it's damned important. In testing, the difference between the right and not right offer is often the difference between success and that really bad place.

The marketing cliché, of course, is "Make them an offer they can't refuse." But it's rarely that simple.

The offer is really about contributing to the sale in the most profitable manner. And not just in the short run. The best offers maximize the value of customer relationships over time.

Optimarketers are keenly aware of offer math. They work it to their advantage. I recently read that the average Kindle owner spends $443 more on Amazon. com each year than the average Amazon.com shopper who doesn't own a Kindle. That's probably why it's been rumored that Amazon earns nothing – or even operates at a slight loss – on each Kindle purchase. They make it up on the back end. The math ultimately works.

Once you understand offer math, you see why "free" offers are used so often. In many cases, a free trial is dramatically more profitable than the usual options. A free offer may yield 10 times the response rate of the next offer option. Will it attract lots of "tire kickers?" In many cases, yes. But very often, free offers also attract dramatically more serious buyers and win by a big margin in bottom-line terms.

A staple of marketing is the money-back guarantee. They're very common among many types of respected businesses. Why? Because they tend to generate revenue far greater than their added expense. They pay out.

If you've wondered about charitable offers, I have some disappointing news from the experience front: In a sweepstakes, when we offered a set of prize options that appealed to each prospect's self-interest and one that gave respondents a chance to make a charitable contribution to a needy kid, fewer than 1% of respondents chose the charitable option.

But that was one test for one marketer. Your results may differ. In fact, I'm sure charitable offers work in other settings and with specific age groups. Millennials, for example, have been strong supporters of social enterprises. Plus, not every marketer who implements a charitable offer cares if it's the most profitable way to go. And in some cases, a charitable-contribution offer may be used as an option for prospects who can't accept a premium or prize due to company policy. Charitable offers are certainly great to test.

Whether it's educational content, discount, freebie, premium, or sweepstakes, it's not as much about running a "relevant" offer as it is about contributing to the ultimate objective. Sometimes we design the offer to entice a subset of solid prospects just so they raise their hands and show interest.

In other cases, the audience consists almost entirely of the right prospects, and it's largely a matter of moving as many as possible downstream. When an offer isn't responsible for helping select the right audience, it may not matter if a premium has no direct link to the product or service.

Sometimes it's important for the offer itself to attract a high percentage of out-standing prospects. Small sales teams that can't afford to be overloaded with tire-kickers, for example, tend to appreciate that approach. As I said, it's com-plicated. And worthwhile to test your way to your own success.

Now let's talk about offers used by great database marketers. These folks live off relevant prospect and customer information; the richer the feedback collected, the higher the value of the database. Extremely enticing (but highly cost-ef-fective) offers give marketers a chance to collect more relevant feedback from prospects. If I want you to answer six questions on the landing page, I'm more likely to get you to comply by waving a gift card in front of you.

On that note, it's important to merchandise your offers properly. As I said, early on, when we began experimenting with a hybrid of interesting concepts and textbook response marketing techniques, we quickly discovered that if we cranked up the volume on the concept too much at the expense of the offer, we took a response-rate hit. Ultimately, it was best to push both offer *and* con-cept simultaneously. Think of it as direct marketing orthodoxy meets Madison Avenue.

A hotly debated marketing topic is whether it pays to give prospects a choice (e.g., "choose from these premiums"). Yes, sometimes you have no choice but to offer ... a choice. Here's what we've learned: A choice of offers is often counterproductive (and even deadly). The marketer loses the opportunity for singularity. When it looks like you're about to force the viewer to work harder, it's worth stopping and asking whether it's best to go another route.

The best protection – and a way to gain an edge over competitors – is to test offers. Aggressively. Many marketers should test as many as five offers at a time to understand as quickly as possible what works best. It's ideal to test offers ASAP, because back-end results (e.g., conversions) often require weeks, months, or longer.

Many of the best offers are like the best concepts: They're fresh rather than me-too. They're bold and daring and even groundbreaking. Try going all out on an upcoming offer. But if at all possible, do subject it to a controlled test.

CASE EXAMPLE: *PHOTOGRAPHIC* SWEEPSTAKES

When I worked in circulation promotion for Petersen Publishing, we ran a sweepstakes that's an excellent example of the power of highly relevant offers. Before nailing down a prize structure for a *Photographic* magazine sweepstakes, we solicited ideas from the experts: the magazine's editors. Relevance to photographers was essential; Petersen was obviously in no position to compete with multi-million dollar lotteries. We settled on a choice of dream camera packages for serious photographers. Result: 31% of prospects responded and about one-fourth – almost 8% of the total audience – took a subscription. The sweepstakes offer pulled a 7.97% subscriber rate; a non-sweepstakes offer pulled a 2.62% rate. So the sweeps lifted the subscriber rate by 204%. We needed 24,000 subscriptions and pulled in more than 32,000. Never underestimate the power of a super relevant offer. And when you use one, don't bury it. Lead with it.

WHAT'S FASCINATING ABOUT THE "CALL TO ACTION"

The call to action is simply what you request of prospects as a next step. Fascinating thing about it: Very often, simply by asking people to do what you want them to do, they do it – and you raise the response rate. So if you're hoping prospects fill out your easy-to-complete landing page form, try saying something like "Complete this easy form now." Want people to order sooner rather than later? Say something like "Order by April 30 and save 10%."

During this year's Oscars broadcast, host Ellen DeGeneres took a star-studded selfie, posted it on Twitter, and asked viewers to retweet it to set a retweet record. They did precisely that – simply because Ellen asked.

Call-to-action optimization won't make an enormous difference, but it's an easy way to raise outcomes.

SOURCE CODES TRANSFORM MARKETING PROFITS

Forgive the cliché I'm about to share, as it's a propos: You can't manage what you can't measure. Marketers who track results by source know which sources are – and aren't – doing well. With that knowledge, they're able to shift marketing spending to the most productive sources and away from unproductive ones.

Don't let the semi-fancy term "source code" scare you: Your unique landing page URL linked to a Google AdWords ad is a source code. As is a designated toll-free number you place in a radio spot on Kiss 108. Not to mention a numeric code you affix to a postal mailer near each recipient's address.

In many cases, it's impossible to track 100% of results back to original sources. But that doesn't mean you shouldn't try to track as much of your marketing as possible by source – and assign related revenues and marketing expenses over time to those sources for an ROI calculation. Even with social media, it may be possible to pull this off to a meaningful degree.

Let's say your company has a LinkedIn group. John Drake became a member. When John landed in your database, your company had no prior record of him. Several months after being added, John becomes a customer. It's reasonable for your LinkedIn group to receive credit for that relationship.

Yes, things won't always be that obvious, and the group may at times be responsible for an "assist." But we've made important decisions – with profound bottom-line impact – after accurately tracking roughly 70% of results.

Today you hardly ever hear John Wanamaker's famous line "Half the money I spend on advertising is wasted; the trouble is I don't know which half." For most marketers, that no longer has to be the case.

Knowing how each of your customer sources contribute to your bottom line could be a major driver of your success as a marketer. Act as if source codes are critically important. Because they are.

THE BEST MARKETERS ARE THE BEST TESTERS

I've worked closely with nearly 150 businesses and observed hundreds of others. I'll say this: The majority of marketers don't run enough tests – and many that test regularly don't run enough important ones.

The best marketers tend to be the best testers. Testing is to marketing what research and development is to manufacturing. Rather than make decisions based on opinions, speculation, and biases, marketers who regularly test work with facts.

It's never been easier and cheaper for marketers to run good tests. Take Google AdWords. In seconds, you're able to structure A/B tests (the same variable tested in two ways) and even pull off A/B/C/D tests. And in some cases do it for under $100.

When the sample size of a test is big enough, marketers may obtain a sufficient number of responses and declare a winner within days or even hours. But it's important to secure projectable results. Through testing, Optimarketers often operate at a 90% or better confidence level, with a small "limit of error."

You want to nail the mechanics of testing, but there's more to the craft than that. Optimarketers operate in a culture of experimentation. It's safe for them to fail. In fact, regular failure should be the expectation.

It pays to be a nurturer of experimentation. Marketers regularly run excellent tests in supportive environments. Surest way to shut down experimentation:

Make people believe their tests had better succeed – or else.

In many cases, one successful rollout will pay for 10 losers. Joe Sugarman, who became an immensely successful direct marketer with products like BluBlocker sunglasses, told me "I have failed more times than anybody I have ever known."

Recently, Megan McArdle wrote an acclaimed book on succeeding through serial failure. It's called *The Upside of Down: Why Failing Well Is the Key to Success.*

Measurable marketers minimize risk by limiting initial circulation to only what's needed to yield projectable results. Nothing more. After results arrive, we roll out winners unchanged and change or eliminate losers.

But not all losing test categories should be permanently eliminated. For example, virtually every business needs inbound marketing (marketing that pulls in prospects and customers via content, organic search, and other non-outbound means). So if an initial test of inbound marketing fails, it's best to stay with it.

After test results arrive, winners roll out with all variables that were in place under the test – only using larger circulation. This means a "control" (winning) approach may run for months or even years.

A classic mistake among marketers is testing insignificant elements. When you test things that make little difference, you're likely to see little difference in results. Put another way, insignificant changes tend to result in insignificant change.

To borrow from baseball, Optimarketers "swing for the fences." They test big elements – including creative, media, and offer.

By all means, test red vs. green as a color, but only after you've stepped through experiments with greater potential impact. Be sure to prioritize your tests.

And test regularly. When I worked on massive consumer direct mail campaigns early in my career, we were taught that every major mailing should have at least one test. That advice applies to major campaigns in all media.

Whatever you do, don't think other marketers' experiences can replace your need to test. When I was employed on the client side, we watched as competitors imitated our marketing – including using untested tactics in place for ages on our list of items to test for ourselves.

Remember this hard-won lesson: It's generally far easier to improve a successful marketing program than to revive a dead one. So test while you're on top. Don't wait till your outcomes tank.

When you run a test, make it count. Do it right. Take steps to avoid a blown test that produces worthless or even misleading results. Don't be left second-guessing whether a proper test could have yielded a better outcome.

How should you respond if a boss says he hired you to know answers in advance? Help him lose the notion that one marketer replaces the need for regular testing.

Explain that great marketers don't have all the answers, but know which questions to ask and which hypotheses to form. If the boss is mathematically inclined, justify testing in mathematical terms. It's hard to debate whether a test should run when it's presented as a reasonable approach to raising profits. More on that later.

A military veteran once said testing is like "cracking the code." I always liked that.

CASE EXAMPLE: TEST OF SOLO VS. OMNIBUS AD

When I managed the Publishers Choice business unit of National Syndications, we bought enormous blocks of remnant space in *Parade* magazine, the Sunday newspaper supplement with circulation of around 32 million. Publishers Choice sold well over 50,000 books a year to woodworkers alone.

Because of the huge commitments we made, we had to test constantly to avoid losing our shirts on any given Sunday. We tested products, concepts, full-page vs. half-page ads, prices, add-on offers, headlines, short vs. long copy, color vs. black and white, among other elements.

Of course, we had zero ability to select readers with specific woodworking interests from circulation north of 30 million. So the protocol had been to run omnibus ads containing a full set of woodworking books designed to appeal to a wide range of interests.

But then we did something some marketers might consider counterintuitive: test a proven omnibus ad against a top-selling (but narrowly focused) woodworking title: *Scroll Saw Pattern Book*. Because we had a full page available for the single title, we were able to go with longer copy, which is useful in one-step selling. We also had room to show several examples of scroll saw patterns.

Result: The omnibus ad achieved a return on promotional investment (ROPI) of -12%; the solo ad yielded a ROPI of +92%. When we saw findings like that, the president of National Syndications would say "What do we know? We don't know nuthin'." Marketing is a business of surprises. Test liberally.

OPTIMAL WAY TO IDENTIFY THE OPTIMAL CAMPAIGN

Until now, major marketers have often relied on primary and secondary research on the front end when developing campaigns – and then made a big speculative leap when going live. In many cases, they've brought together small numbers of focus group participants – people sitting alongside each other with a moderator.

Sometimes participants' answers to questions had little to do with reality. When you seat people next to each other in an artificial environment, they often give socially acceptable answers. Who wants to admit they're dumb enough to fall for marketing tactics?

It should be no surprise that people in a focus group who say "That would be a no-brainer for me – I'd absolutely buy it" would never actually do so in real life.

Live testing has always been better than focus group testing (and better than focus group testing combined with popular forms of quantitative research).

But marketers have been reluctant to test very different campaign directions in the real world, for fear of seeming, for lack of a better term, schizophrenic.

Understandably so. But consumers aren't really all that interested in whether a marketer is testing multiple creative directions in the real world. And besides,

57

it's easy to confine the sample size to only what's needed to yield projectable results.

So yes, in live testing, a few prospects may see very different creative directions for a brief time period, but the trade-off is well worth it.

CASE EXAMPLE: STRAIGHTERLINE

StraighterLine offers online, high-quality college courses at a fraction of the cost of traditional colleges. From 300+ raw ideas, we worked up more than 20 potential campaign directions for this marketer. StraighterLine couldn't decide between three of them. So rather than speculate, we tested all three directions against their control approach in web banner advertising. Result: The difference in product trials between the old approach and our highest-pulling new approach was 396%. A live test of concepts in the real world is fast, cheap, and accurate.

BEATING YOUR CURRENT APPROACH

Direct marketers call current advertising the "control." As you may have guessed, the term is derived from controlled testing. Serious testers treat a control like a boxing champion: It remains reining champ till it's beaten in testing or retired.

It's worth spending a moment on the latter because very often, marketers get tired of successful advertising before the public does, and replace superior ads with inferior ones for arbitrary reasons (that said, digital marketers often have the opportunity for high frequency in a short timeframe; in these cases, responsiveness of ads may quickly degrade). Excellent direct marketers, on the other hand, retire a control only when it's no longer profitable.

Beating a control approach may not be easy. Some have stood for months, years, or more than a decade and withstood numerous challenges. To my knowledge, the longest-running control ad was written by Maxwell Sackheim for the Sherwin Cody School of English. The headline read "Do You Make These Mistakes in English?" It ran for more than 40 years.

So what does it take to defeat a control approach, including one that has repeatedly won in testing? It's about adding, subtracting, and leaving certain things as they are.

Yep, it's largely that simple. Find a new dimension to include, remove what's counterproductive or not essential, and keep what's good. But be careful: It's easy to cut into bone and eliminate productive elements. Of course, this can be avoided by testing one variable at a time. So if you're wondering if the offer is optimal, test a new offer while keeping all other elements the same.

You could certainly test more than one variable at once without isolating each variable, but you won't know exactly which variables contributed to a change in the outcome. However, you will know if Alternative A beat Alternative B. Sometimes, accelerated testing of this nature makes a lot of sense – even if you're unable to isolate the contribution of individual elements. That can always come later.

While reviewing my files for this book, I found a list I created more than 20 years ago called "How to Beat the Control." I didn't want to load this book up with lists, but I'll make an exception here, as a hat tip to my younger self. Here it is:

How to Beat the Control
Elements to review:
- Relevance
- Positioning
- Responsiveness of elements vs. cost
- Unique Selling Proposition
- Headline
- Offer
- Benefits
- Copy
- Facts/specificity
- Psychological factors (emotion vs. intellect)
- Scientific factors
- Credibility (including substantiation of claims)
- Testimonials
- Ease of response
- Urgency
- Guarantee
- Tonality
- Art direction
- Personalization

-Involvement device
-Exclusivity
-News
-Perceived ease

CASE EXAMPLE: DR. SOLOMON'S

Dr. Solomon's was a British-based anti-virus company we launched in the United States. The team in the United Kingdom had a marketing program they felt quite good about. But their U.S.-based marketing leader, Anne Beitel, thought it might not do as well as a high-quality marketing program created by a team on this side of the pond. So she proposed a split-run test of the UK work vs. ours. Result: Work developed by our team won by a margin well in the double digits. Naturally, we continued to create marketing for Dr. Solomon's. The company was later sold for more than $600 million.

Projectable split-run test results generally end all arguments.

THE CASE FOR ACCELERATED LEARNING

Optimarketers tend to be impatient. In three months, they step through tests ordinary marketers require three years or more to run.

Think about the bottom-line difference. The marketer needing 1,100% more time to do the same testing as the Optimarketer runs inferior marketing nearly three years longer. Total testing cost is comparable for both marketers. So we're talking about not just a potentially significant bottom-line difference, but possibly the difference between chronic underperformance and serial success.

ABOUT THAT GUY ASKING FOR GUARANTEED SUCCESS

A particularly challenging moment for marketers is when an executive outside marketing says something like "We'll gladly fund the marketing you're proposing ... if you guarantee success."

Optimarketers can often come close to making a guarantee. A 95% confidence level that a rollout will be within 10% of a test result is damned close to that. But executives seeking guarantees are often talking about the initial marketing investment. When no testing history is available, one can't make any guarantee in good faith.

But that hasn't stopped some marketers from making such guarantees. Those who do either don't understand marketing or aren't being honest.

Executives asking for guarantees should recognize that marketing is a microcosm of business. A new marketing program is in many respects similar to a new business venture. We all know new businesses aren't guaranteed to succeed; they're built on trial and error. Strong managers do their best to maximize the odds of success. Marketers with great track records simply improve the odds.

Executives who want guarantees before funding businesses – or marketing programs – should put their money elsewhere. Treasury bills are guaranteed to perform at a particular level – a low level in comparison to many business opportunities.

If executives don't consider a T-bill ROI acceptable, they need to incur more risk. But they shouldn't expect the basics of business not to apply in the marketing arena. Or to see exceptional returns without risk.

THE ESSENTIAL ROLE OF TECHNOLOGY – AND A WORD OF CAUTION

Evolved marketers are, of course, like other evolved humans: They make damned good use of available tools.

So it should be no surprise that Optimarketers are heavily into technology. (I dictated the first draft of *Optimarketing: Marketing Optimization to Electrify Your Business* using Dragon Dictate voice recognition technology.)

Marketing technology allows us to perform essential chores faster and do things previously considered difficult or impossible. We now can automate a large chunk of marketing.

With this technology, you automate triggered email campaigns, lead scoring, and even the handoff of leads to sales. Using cookies, you see how database prospects respond to your advertising and behave on your website. Previously, these website visits were generally anonymous. But when this behavior becomes known, marketing gets better.

Segmentation, split-run testing, and tracking results all become easier. Technology gives us insights into the interests of prospects and customers in ways that were unthinkable even a decade ago.

Hubspot is a good illustration of what this technology delivers for marketers. The company wrote the book on inbound marketing (it's *Inbound Marketing: Get Found Using Google, Social Media, and Blogs*).

In one integrated platform, Hubspot sorts tools into three groups: attracting visitors, converting leads, and closing customers. Features span social media management, search engine optimization, email marketing, landing pages, website visitor tracking, and a lot more.

A worthwhile business that follows Hubspot's playbook is quite likely to be successful in inbound marketing. And with an entry-level price of $200 a month, it's easy for the payoff to be outstanding.

If you're developing a short list of marketing automation suppliers, besides Hubspot, other highly regarded resources include Act-On, Eloqua (now part of Oracle), Marketo, Pardot (now part of Salesforce), Sugar, and Unica (now part of IBM). Disclosure: Eloqua and Unica have been clients of our agency.

Whether it's Google Hangouts, Pinterest, Instagram, iPhone apps, or Facebook events, Optimarketers use today's tools in exciting ways to find, engage, and convert prospects. Every marketer should regularly think about potential possibilities.

It's worth repeating: Technology is essential for Optimarketers. But I must point out a problem relating to marketing technology users: Too many plumbers and not enough architects.

Some marketers apparently think their job is largely about operating a set of tools. A good number of marketing managers behave like glorified IT people. Why? Because it's what they know; it's where they feel comfortable. They're a bit like the kid who's strong in math but deficient in other essential areas, and as a result, focuses on math.

Marketers in this category need to expand their horizons.

Technology is only one variable. Yep – it's important. But great marketing

66

outcomes are about much more than technology.

Among other things, marketing is also about ideas. Collaboration. Research. Conceptualization. Design. Storytelling. Offers. Experimentation. Media. Salesmanship.

It's tragic to see marketers scoring very high on the technology front but operating in a mediocre manner in other key areas. They're like the student with one "A" and four "Cs."

Optimarketers go for straight "As."

WHERE EVENT MARKETERS SHOULD GO FROM HERE

Major event marketers tend to nail the fundamentals. Many have embraced new tools and techniques. But event marketing needs an upgrade. It's often too boilerplate. Unimaginative. Ordinary.

Let's start with the front end: In many cases, web-based research aimed at prospects can quickly and inexpensively identify the best topics, speakers, venues, and more, to raise demand. Event marketers should use it more often.

An example: Some time ago, a marketer I know and respect started managing events for an association. He began using web-based research to rank prospects' interest in various topics. The not-surprising result: Demand instantly began rising. Instead of rubber-stamping preferences of association leaders and potential speakers, this marketer used a more methodical and quantitative approach.

As for event titles, they often seem as if they were contemplated for less than 30 seconds. The title is obviously a key element and worthy of more consideration, to say the least.

And why is the event ad's headline often the ... event title? Event prospects aren't much different from other prospects. They'll respond to emotional appeals within relevant, smart, and even unconventional concepts. Among other things, the headline is a chance to create a sense of excitement.

Bullet points have their place, but shouldn't be used simply to minimize time required to promote an event. Marketers are storytellers. Our job is to win prospects over. It's time for many event marketers to think beyond bullet points and embrace an age-old source of a competitive edge: high-quality copywriting.

One invaluable tool that's largely been underutilized in event marketing is web video. Speakers (or others) could give a sneak preview. Video could also be used for conceptual presentations – even super-relevant TV-style commercials.

And of course, social media should be optimized. Cool event pages and groups could be launched to sharpen speaker presentations; answer questions; build a sense of anticipation and community among participants; and raise demand.

Many event marketers now rely heavily on email marketing. Email often consists of the event title as headline; day, time, and location; a set of bullet points; brief speaker bio; and "Click Now." Boilerplate marketing of this nature may carry a substantial opportunity cost.

Standard event marketing should be reimagined. If you think you're doing extremely well with what you have, try cutting your prospect list in half, testing two different treatments, and tracking results.

CASE EXAMPLE: AMERICAN MANAGEMENT ASSOCIATION

Once upon a time, I managed a 120-page American Management Association course catalog. Covers had traditionally featured a montage of different areas of AMA training (e.g., manufacturing, finance, sales). We decided to shake things up, starting with a catalog redesign that showcased a gorgeous aerial shot of the New York Marathon (AMA was headquartered in the Big Apple) on the cover. AMA events really had little to do with marathons, but the photo seemed to fit. That catalog achieved the highest return on marketing investment up until then. Later, we decided to challenge, via split-run testing, the widespread belief that discounts wouldn't lift B2B seminar response rates. As an urgency incentive, we offered a discount to those who registered by a particular date. A surprise

69

to many: The test offer with the discount lifted the response rate enough to make it the winner. Go figure.

Question everything.

OPTIMARKETING AND MOBILITY

How many people under age 30 do you know who *don't* carry a smartphone? Unless you've been living off the grid for a decade or more, you're aware of the proliferation of mobile computing – and the need to be where your users are.

Smartphones, tablets, e-readers – they present big opportunities and big challenges for marketers. Many interfaces are a small fraction of the size of desktop computers. Advertising space is often a tiny fraction of traditional interface space.

It's essential for your communications to look good on mobile devices. Start with your website. In recent years, it's become easy to have a website play well on a full range of devices. A good example is responsive web design, a design approach that optimizes each viewer's experience, regardless of interface. When WordPress users search for a new website theme to use as a building block, they typically see a selection of responsive web design themes that automatically look good on a wide variety of popular devices.

Alpha Software, a firm that's been a client of our agency, has a product called Alpha Anywhere that enables HTML5 applications to look excellent on everything from iPhones to Dell desktop PCs. It's ideal for data-intensive applications, including GPS-enabled ones.

Possibilities for creating meaningful mobile experiences are exciting. You can deliver an entertaining and relevant video or educational podcast series for a full range of mobile users. Even the smallest business can build mobile apps

71

without any technical skills whatsoever.

Marketers are now able to engage with customers and prospects while they're enjoying breakfast, commuting to work, or exercising. When you're at the top of your game, people may consider your content more interesting than what's on TV.

Whether it's SMS (text messaging) updates, a full-blown mobile app, or a Kindle e-book, Optimarketers give people what they want – where they want it.

A mobile strategy is no longer nice to have. It's essential.

OPTIMIZING WITH "TOUCH POINTS"

When I was a little guy, a toupée company owner in the New York metropolitan area regularly appeared in his own TV commercials. He'd make big claims, jump in a pool wearing a wig, and say "I wouldn't mislead you for a very good reason. I'm the president of the company."

Strange twist: I believe Morrie in "Goodfellas" was based on that owner. Not exactly an honest businessman. But back then, people believed claims from seemingly accomplished executives. Today, not so much.

Honorable marketers pay for the misdeeds of dishonest ones. It's a bit like the attitude a spurned lover may bring to the next suitor. Your prospects have bought products and services that didn't live up to expectations. They've been burned – repeatedly. By the time they hear from you, they're hardened skeptics.

It's reasonable to start with the assumption that prospects don't believe your marketing claims. So how do you maximize credibility in an age of skepticism?

For openers, it helps to tell the truth – consistently – using fact- and evidence-based presentations. What if you don't have strong substantiation for your claims? Go out and get it.

Some sales reps (and their bosses) think the right prospects will hear a pitch for the first time and instantly roll over. It happens ... in some instances, with a small percentage of prospects.

But it's important to respect the natural sales process. We've advised marketers to not push prospects toward "unnatural acts." If about 100% of prospects won't be prepared for an in-person meeting after initially responding to your appeal, don't try to force it.

Consider the romance analogy. Most people wouldn't think of proposing marriage after one date. In some cases, a couple have 100 dates (or whatever you want to call them) before they're engaged.

In short, it's best not to ask your prospects to do things they wouldn't naturally do.

In the real world, prospects often convert after multiple "touches." Some prospects will convert after five touches; others will need more than 50. A client at a large software company once told us they had concluded that eight touches were necessary before they had any reason to expect to hear from a prospect.

Many prospects really, truly need nurturing. An email campaign to the database that unveils key benefits, problems solved, and case examples – and gradually builds an excellent case for buying – will tend to make a significant difference. Especially if it's imaginative, relevant, captivating, smart – and present when prospects decide they need you. It pays to go the distance with your nurture program and make it exceptional.

But relationship-building is about more than lead nurture via email. Social media, used properly, may bring prospects over to your side at a highly efficient rate. Your posts on Twitter, LinkedIn, Facebook, and other social sites can enable you and your business to go from stranger to trusted resource.

Whether it's lead nurture, social networking, or other forms of marketing, Optimarketers behave like human beings on every touch point. Each post feels like it's from a person, not a company. Let's talk about that a bit more.

GET (MORE) REAL

Ever notice how popular music has grown more authentic over the years? Listen to The Everly Brothers' "Bye Bye Love" and Alanis Morissette's "You Oughta Know" back-to-back and you notice more is revealed in the latter. Much more. It's a trend that's continued for decades.

Marketing, as well, keeps growing more authentic. But many marketers still reveal relatively little in their marketing – and of themselves in social media.

Mari Smith is one of the most respected Facebook experts on the planet. If you want to see how an amazing marketer shares her fascinating life with the world while educating prospects, building her business, and having a blast, follow Mari on the Social Network.

Now let's look at a common phenomenon. An important phrase is attributed to adman Nick Pisacane: The mask of the advertiser.

Marketers often act as if they're wearing a mask. Claims are so unbelievable, they're not to be believed. Read aloud their copy and you get the impression you're hearing from a company instead of people.

The problem isn't confined to advertising. On social media, many marketing executives keep their guard up to an excessive degree. Fearful of missteps, they reveal little of their true selves. As a result, they're less interesting and often, well … kinda boring. They attract fewer followers and of those they attract, few care to engage with them.

Granted, the CMO of a public company may rightfully feel inclined to be more cautious than the marketing manager in a tiny startup. But many marketers can – and should – stretch more. Not just in social media, but in advertising and even in business meetings, to produce more valuable work.

Being genuine sells more effectively. It's also a more rewarding way to live.

CONTENT RULES

The oft-cited cliché "content is king" isn't much of a stretch.

Marketers are ultimately out to sell, but it can't be done very well by constantly making sales pitches. Consumers can simply step away from that TV spot, ignore that banner ad, turn that magazine page, or opt-out of that email series.

So we educate, entertain, or both. We tell stories. Professional storyteller and longtime friend Lisa Lipkin says:

"Since man's earliest days on earth, stories have been central to communication. Preliterate cultures understood how to demand attention, make information stick, use narratives to persuade, seduce, entertain, and call people to action. In many ways, our society today demands those same skills. In an age of ailing attention spans, a disinterest in reading, and an inability to stay in the moment, now more than ever we need to conjure up the storytelling skills of the ancients."

When marketers are really smart about it, they share stories in ways that advance their business. We gain permission to frequently touch prospects and customers in meaningful ways – even multiple times a day. But in return, marketers are expected to not abuse that privilege and provide (forgive the trite term) value.

Providing value isn't about inducing boredom; it's about creating unique, highly relevant experiences that matter. Getting beyond ordinary is never easy. It starts with where a business is vs. where it wants to be: goals and objectives, as well as strategies and tactics to get there. Too often, marketing content is insufficiently strategic, not prioritized, and misaligned with business goals. Some marketers merely create content within their comfort zone – or worse, based on their own interests and pursuits, rather than on customer needs and wants.

If you rely on leads, marketing content is hugely important. Lead generation is heavily dependent on calls to action with compelling offers – including offers of educational content. The unwritten agreement between seller and buyer: Give up a little information on yourself and get something you want in return.

Marketers should, as quickly as possible, experiment with an appropriately wide variety of content types, to arrive at the optimal content mix. A mix in marketing is usually best (see "Shortcomings of Putting All Eggs in One Basket") – and it's *always* best to know what's engaging prospects and helping them convert.

Remember this: Optimizing your content volume, mix, forms/landing pages, promotion, and tracking could raise your quantity of qualified leads dramatically.

Content marketing success is indeed about *volume* to a substantial degree. So start producing lots of relevant content, get it out there, and keep score.

You can develop content for owned (e.g., your website), paid (e.g., search marketing), and earned (e.g., blogs not owned by you) media. Employees can share it with social media connections. Sales reps can offer it to named accounts. You'll find no shortage of uses for your marketing content.

Your content should be relevant to people at various stages of the buying process. The person shopping for a subcompact car should see very different content than the owner of a brand-spanking-new Mini Cooper.

As a marketer, you can tap a variety of relevant resources to make your content seemingly ubiquitous: your website and email nurture program; social sites like Twitter, LinkedIn, YouTube, Facebook, Pinterest, Instagram, and Google+. As well as a range of online publications, including blogs.

Sophisticated marketers talk about converged media: leveraging two or more owned, paid, or earned media options in a consistent and seamless manner across media and devices. Business author Tim Ferriss has called this "surround sound." It's a potent way to break through and stay top-of-mind.

Don't play small ball when it comes to your marketing content. Aim for awesomeness. Be methodical. Work from a content calendar. Optimize each content placement to draw in as many of the right viewers as possible. (Yes, make sure someone sweats details like meta descriptions.)

Why not ask yourself "What if we create a content marketing program so outstanding, people actually crave it?"

CASE EXAMPLE: CENTERLINE SOFTWARE

In the early days of object-oriented software development, developers were reluctant to embrace objects, which represented a new way of working – and thinking. CenterLine made programming environments for cutting-edge software developers. To offer prospects content that would contribute to sales, content creators studied development teams already working in an object-oriented manner within a CenterLine programming environment. One observation: Early adapters developed a piece of an application in an object-oriented way as a pilot, rather than a full application. By showing how early adapters were becoming successful in the real world with objects and demystifying what was truly a new paradigm, lots of new teams jumped onboard and software development changed forever. I'm proud that our agency played a role in an important educational campaign.

THE MEDIUM IS MORE THAN THE MESSAGE

A maxim worth sharing: Put decent creative work in front of an ideal audience and you may do reasonably well or even better. But put amazing creative before the wrong audience and your outcome will absolutely, positively suck.

In most cases, to succeed in measurable terms, you don't need an audience consisting entirely of the right prospects. It largely comes down to your cost per contact: The higher the cost per contact, the lower the acceptable waste level, and vice versa.

Direct mail, with a relatively high cost per contact, demands minimal waste. But television advertising, with a much lower cost per contact, is often successful when a tiny share of the audience fits the profile for the advertiser's offering.

Ever see a TV ad asking if you were injured in a car accident? (I know – production quality was probably cheesy.) Anyway, that personal injury lawyer may have needed only one new client to consider the effort very profitable. But if he tried the same approach to a similar audience using direct mail at an exponentially higher cost per contact, the outcome, from a bottom-line standpoint, could have been much worse.

Many marketers with substantial inbound marketing programs still spend large sums on outbound marketing (one reason: to distribute marketing content more widely). But doesn't that qualify as "interruption marketing?" Yep – the same marketing that keeps producing excellent profits for many of the world's most successful brands. If outbound marketing works, Optimarketers tend to use it. And if organic forms of inbound marketing prove far superior, they give them a bigger piece of the marketing pie.

It's easy for media, including cost-per-click options like Google AdWords, to represent a large chunk of the marketing programs budget. So it's vital to understand as quickly as possible which media works – and which doesn't.

You want to approach media without biases. In marketing, it's common for managers to stick with media they've used in the past – and understand. But what actually works from a bottom-line standpoint may be very different. Some marketers have a bias toward offline marketing. Or inbound. Or pay-per-click. Those biases could cause expensive mistakes to be made.

Optimarketers run the right tests – ASAP – and make decisions based on actual "dollar votes." No, you probably can't test every interesting media option at the same time. But it's a good idea to step through your important tests as fast as you can.

One way to quickly and efficiently test media options is to take a category approach to testing. Ed Nash, my former boss at BBDO Direct, introduced me to this methodology.

You begin by ranking your media categories – and then rank alternatives within each. Categories deemed to have a bigger potential payoff and higher odds of success get a larger share of initial spending. After testing begins, you quickly wade more deeply into successful categories and eliminate unsuccessful ones.

Something you don't want to do: Drop good money on a dreadful media property. Fortunately, many of the worst offenders telegraph their shortcomings. Biggest signal that it's best to avoid that media buy: When a list owner or broker says "We can't reveal the source." That's a nearly 100% guarantee it'll never pay. When it comes to the all-important media piece, always know what you're getting into.

And know what's working early on, when learning is relatively cheap. After spending a small fortune on media over several years, you don't want to find out that something you could have tried much sooner was in fact your most productive source. It's best to run small-scale media experiments at the earliest possible time.

Think of your customer sources as buckets. You want to start by optimizing your inbound marketing buckets, but because few things in marketing are truly free, always understand their real cost, to compare against other sources.

With paid media, after testing, place more of your budget into your most productive buckets. Track performance over time to avoid betting heavily on excessively leaky buckets. That's one good way to optimize your marketing mix.

Oh – and what about my headline statement? Marshall McLuhan famously said, "The medium is the message." Each media placement impacts your brand reputation. It's helpful to ask "Is this the right environment for us?" Obviously, an ad on the *Architectural Digest* website makes a different statement than a flyer on windshields. McLuhan was right.

YOUR WEBSITE AS CENTER OF YOUR MARKETING UNIVERSE

That you're reading this tells me you know the digital experience you offer is, to say the least, important. If anything, it's growing more important every year.

Let's face it: Your website has a huge job. It should be a differentiator, educator, lead generator, brand-builder, and more.

Prospects often research businesses online for days, weeks, or months before filling out a registration form or contacting a sales rep. If your competition thrills prospects online to such a degree they don't feel compelled to even contact you, it may not matter if you've got a better mousetrap.

So let's go beyond the obvious and talk about website optimization. It's common practice to write website content around high-priority search terms. There's substantial value in that.

Most websites should have a blog, but marketers shouldn't be slavishly devoted to SEO copy. You never want to become what's known as a "traffic whore." It's important to give customers and prospects differentiated content they *want* to read – with or without major search terms.

Many marketers are now essentially in the publishing business and, if they aren't, they should be. It's frequently an excellent idea to create an online destination that educates in unique ways while advancing the business.

As I've said, marketers should be masterful storytellers, providing abundant value while using content to help the business meet objectives. There's a great – but underutilized – tool to make that happen.

I'm sure you've heard of it: web video. Video exploded on the web after YouTube was launched – and after Forrester Research famously said websites containing video were more than 50 times as likely to appear on page one of Google search results than sites without it.

Video communicates in ways more powerful than other options. Yet in most cases the potential of web video on corporate websites has yet to be realized. Very often, extraordinary web video could be the centerpiece of a home page presentation. It could do an excellent job of educating customers and prospects. And compel many viewers to take that next step.

Your home page starts the buying process. In all forms of advertising, concept quality could be critical to success. Yet many websites lack a concept. Or if they have one, it's nothing to write home about.

Optimarketers care passionately about conceptual quality, to reduce the bounce rate and, more importantly, maximize website revenue. Your home page should rock prospects out of their complacency.

One way to make this happen is by being extremely relevant from the get-go. It's easy to offer different content for viewers in different segments of your audience. And with tools like Hubspot, you're able to dynamically serve different content for, say, prospects vs. leads.

Excellent content will undoubtedly take you a long way. It's likely to get you external links to your site – and thus, improved search rankings – but you'll want to make other moves to ensure that search engines pick up on the outstanding work you're doing. SEO remains a moving target, but as of this moment, things like short (as well as keyword-rich) permalink URLs, logical outbound links, and social sharing buttons still help. It's important to continually incorporate what's working in SEO.

Something more marketers should explore: microsites. These are relatively modest websites with an extra dimension of specificity. They may be used for a particular campaign, promotion, product, event, cause, or opportunity. Microsites are a chance to stretch a brand using an unconventional concept, URL, video, game – you name it.

All this brings us to what many online marketers care about most: Forms completed. Leads generated. Trials started. Sales initiated.

Many websites could do a much better job of merchandising offers. Very often, this should happen right from the home page. You could experiment with offers for prospects at different phases of the buying process, to collect feedback from a higher percentage of visitors. To optimize website lead generation, it's worth testing variations in offers, feedback collection, form structure, landing pages, and more.

FROM "SELL, SELL, SELL" TO SMART USE OF SOCIAL MEDIA

Shortly after grown-ups were allowed on Facebook, our agency launched a Facebook group called "What I Saw at the Direct Marketing Revolution." We thought the name would attract innovative marketers who'd be candidates for our shop. And I figured the experience would be fun.

We began starting conversations on measurable marketing that weren't available anywhere else. Not only did people begin posting; some became passionate about discussions and remained very active.

It was a group we created and managed, so we could have posted each day about our agency's services. But that would have turned members off – and they probably would have slammed us on Facebook as well. We kept things educational.

Before long, our strategy paid off. Within several months of launching the group, we obtained two clients directly from it. Prior to their inquiries we never gave a sales pitch – they just participated in conversations, enjoyed the discussions, scoped us out when they needed help, liked what they saw, contacted us, and became clients.

It was monetization of social media before it was cool (this was before Facebook pages even existed). The great lesson we picked up from that early experience: Turning social media into a genuine moneymaker isn't as mysterious as some people think.

Start by setting objectives – what you want out of it, in measurable and non-measurable terms. Review the relevant landscape, not just in social media but in more traditional vehicles too. Study businesses in your space you respect, not to ape them, but with an eye toward exceeding their efforts.

Take stock: Think about what you and your team could uniquely contribute in social media. From there, it should be fairly easy to know which social media properties make the most sense (e.g., whether or not you should launch a LinkedIn group) and what to do within them.

An interesting question to ask: What if we aim to bring together a group of people with a shared interest or passion for an experience unlike any other?

You want customers and prospects to learn from you and engage with you, and as a result, become more likely to buy from you. It largely comes down to producing excellent content, consistently.

Consistency is important; posting regularly helps you attract a larger audience and keep them engaged. In some cases, community members will contribute the lion's share of content. And of course, on social sites like LinkedIn, Twitter, and Facebook, you'll have the opportunity to promote your posts and dramatically hike exposure.

Being exceptional in social media means putting aside the "sell, sell, sell" mentality of the past. It's not simply about what the sales team prefers. A selfish perspective won't cut it. People don't want to be pitched.

Customer interests should be Priority #1.

In social media, educational content will almost always beat brochureware. But ya know what? If you regularly add value, you'll be able to periodically sell – overtly – at the right times and to the right people (e.g., those near the bottom of your marketing funnel). In fact, many prospects and customers will figure all that excellent content comes at a small price: the understanding that periodically you'll hawk your wares in appropriate ways.

Great social media users don't engage in "black hat" magic. Google has said for years that marketers don't need double-secret SEO tricks to rank high on their search engine. Early on, it was largely an aspirational statement by the Sultans of Search. But today it's finally true. It's mostly a matter of offering visitors an excellent experience by regularly serving relevant, compelling content people want to view – and share.

Optimarketers get this done using the best and most relevant tools available – including web video, content curation, and different types of graphic presentations (the latter are usually shared more often than straight text).

A community is only as good as its members. To acquire the right members, consider testing a range of media (e.g., your internal email list, search marketing, Facebook or LinkedIn ads). If it produces a great ROI it's the right thing to do.

As social media expert and friend Roger Harris has pointed out, it's often a good idea to actively recruit people through personal contact you think will make an outstanding contribution to your social networking group.

Success in social media means going beyond your own sites to other destinations where you and your team provide value by joining discussions, answering questions, and sharing relevant content.

Social media takes time. Many marketers need to dedicate a person or entire team to make the most of it. In smaller operations, a marketing staff member should spend at least an hour a day on social media.

But remember, this is strategic, so don't simply turn everything over to 20-somethings (even if they're smarter than you in key respects). Highly experienced marketers should stay actively involved.

You can't be everywhere on social media – nor should you be. So think of platforms and sites that matter most and focus on them. Treat these destinations as interdependent resources. They should support each other (e.g., your YouTube channel feeds content to your Facebook page). Measure how you're doing to keep getting better.

For many businesses, all of this should go hand-in-hand with social selling. Social selling is about using social media to close more business. Bearing little resemblance to traditional selling, people engaged in social selling lead with value – and operate with more patience than traditional sales reps.

Whether it's on Twitter, Quora, or LinkedIn, social sellers weave their products and services into exchanges only when appropriate. But of course, when prospects ask to engage directly with a rep as part of a buying decision, they're right there.

Your educational content is a chance to impact prospects at all stages of the buying process. Important, because that viewer of your video with no current plans to buy may very well buy from you 15 months from now.

Many businesses should be in the publishing arena and don't even know it. With content curation tools and quality content writers available, more marketers should indeed be publishers. Imagine bringing a serious percentage of your target group together via unique educational content, on a site that becomes a major asset for your business. Hell, you could even run your own house ads. And seriously augment your opt-in email list.

Pawan Deshpande, CEO of Curata, a content curation software business that's worked with our agency, once said content curation is like going to the gym. If you look in the mirror after a day or two, you won't notice a difference. But stay with it and in a reasonable amount of time you'll definitely see significant change.

Great marketers are great listeners. It's important to regularly *listen* to what customers and prospects are saying about your business in social media – and respond appropriately. You'll find no shortage of effective and inexpensive social media monitoring tools.

Social media will help you attract, engage, influence, and stay connected with prospects and customers. By staying on top of your audience and providing serious value in ways true to your brand and aligned with business goals, you'll find social media more than beneficial.

EMAIL: THE UNDERUTILIZED CONCEPTUAL CANVAS

Email marketing transforms the math of relationship-building. Let's look at two key marketing ingredients: reach and frequency. Email marketing extends both.

Using email, for a miniscule fraction of traditional marketing cost, marketers can reach prospects in their marketing database 50 or more times a year (unless they opt-out). This means marketers can focus as never before on the "knowledge" side of marketing and invest in oft-neglected elements like strategy and creativity.

In the early days of email marketing, we realized it was an excellent canvas for creativity. When we began testing HTML against textual email, it was like a clinical trial halted early due to success: The lift from strong conceptual and visual email was that striking.

Shortly afterward, computer security measures left us unable to do some of the cool stuff we did in the early days of email marketing – but fortunately, visual email was never taken off the table.

Because of the medium's limitations, many email marketers retreated and began acting as if email advertising wasn't even advertising. Today, in the third decade of email marketing, we rarely see interesting concepts in our inboxes. This means email marketing remains an open field for Optimarketers. It's a chance to deliver a hybrid that includes excellent conceptual work, strong art direction, and textbook direct marketing.

Besides those elements, your email should reflect "best practices" of the medium. This means avoiding terms often used by spammers and watching the text-to-image ratio (to Internet service providers, image-only email equals spam). Run your images no larger than necessary, to keep from triggering spam filters. Your concept and offer should be viewable on most laptops without scrolling. The first HTML text should be compelling, for recipients who don't see images.

Custom email advertising should be coded by someone who understands email coding (it's different than website coding). It's important to test across a range of web browsers and devices. And it's best to deploy through an email service provider with high deliverability rates.

Optimarketers take advantage of segmentation and personalization in email. Does personalized email really make a difference? Yes, it typically does. Aberdeen found that personalized email improves clickthroughs by 14% and conversion rates by 10%. So if you get the chance, by all means personalize that subject line, salutation, or other area. But also take advantage of data to segment your audience effectively and be as relevant as possible.

Email serves up audience segments for relevant marketing content – including web video, infographics, presentations, games, and more. It beautifully sets up potential engagement on social media. So you want to link to your social sites.

At times you'll identify a range of interesting options in email marketing. When more than one emerges, you may want to conduct a split-run test. Subject lines, concepts, offers, and more are easily tested in email. Because it's a breeze to vary landing page URLs, your tests should be simple to track.

Businesses should pull out all the stops to acquire opt-ins. Stores can hold contests with prizes as a means of acquiring email addresses (a common tactic of trade show exhibitors). And of course, the company website, blog, and other owned online properties are ideal for gaining permission to send email.

Something you absolutely shouldn't do: Make email recipients want to press the "opt-out" button by bombarding them with email and being, well … obnoxious.

Several years ago, I signed up for a low-end product offer. Instantly the company began sending an average of five emails a week. Common sense tells you five-times-a-week frequency is outrageous. (I offered to orchestrate a test of email frequency for this business but they never responded.)

While we're talking about frequency, I should point out that many email marketers don't deploy database email often enough. Messages that appear in inboxes only from time to time appear disconnected; the brand is often forgotten; opportunities to be at the right place at the right time are missed. You don't want to become a stranger in the minds of prospects.

We all know how crowded inboxes are today. How can anyone justify sending perfectly ordinary email advertising? With creativity, yours can convey some of your best marketing ideas ever.

CASE EXAMPLE: *MIT SLOAN MANAGEMENT REVIEW*

Readers of *MIT Sloan Management Review* find no fluff within its pages – just content they need to excel in business management. So we created HTML email advertising featuring a mock cover resembling *People* magazine's "Sexiest Man Alive" issue, only with the title "Sexiest Manager Alive." The headline read "What doesn't go into our magazine is as important as what does." The subhead included a quote from management guru Tom Peters and a complimentary-issue offer. Body copy imaginatively told the MIT SMR story. Result: 29% of recipients who opened the email clicked through to the landing page. Using email, you can – and should – feature surprising, relevant, smart concepts.

TWITTER FOR FUN AND PROFIT

Kim Kardashian has 19.5 million followers on Twitter, a free social media platform. To put this in perspective, daily circulation of *The New York Times*, a company with $343 million in annual operating costs, is 1.9 million.

Twitter is a phenomenon. And a lot of marketers could do much more with it.

For this book's Twitter section, I called Bob Cargill, a longtime friend and social media expert. When I signed up for the Typepad blogging platform back in 2005, I contacted Bob, already a veteran blogger. Bob's blog, *A New Marketing Commentator*, is one of the longest-running marketing blogs. It's also among the best.

During our discussion, we both agreed it's a mistake to buy Twitter followers. Bob pointed out that purchased "followers" could be bots, spammers, or other illegitimate accounts. Better to grow your Twitter following organically. Share knowledge. Engage in conversations – and lead them.

By all means, use Twitter for prospecting by doing searches of keywords, phrases, and hashtags. Use tools like TweetDeck to create a list of people to closely follow. Test Twitter ads to see if they grow your following – and drive business – at an acceptable profit. (It's quite targeted. You can select by interest, company, geography, and more.)

But don't bother with gimmicks. They'll do little or nothing for your business and may even be counterproductive.

Want to be a business celebrity – or simply grow an enviable following? Once again, take stock and think carefully about how you can add value in 140 characters or less per tweet. Bob made an excellent point about being yourself and bringing your personal side into your Twitter handle. Conduct genuine conversations and, when appropriate, do it publicly to share your knowledge. You may raise your Klout score as a result.

Follow the right people. Learn what they're passionate about – what they're sharing. Give them real value and they'll support you. Retweet their valuable contributions you consider relevant to your followers. Direct message them when it genuinely makes sense.

Use hashtags to organize tweets by topic. Entertain followers if you think you should. Share your Twitter handle liberally.

Do all this and you probably won't have, like Kim, millions of people hanging on your every tweet. But you will become an influencer and derive serious benefits from Twitter.

ON THE PUSH TO GET MORE FACEBOOK "LIKES"

Marketers often ask "How do we get more 'likes' on Facebook?"

I recently saw a company selling 10,000 Facebook "likes" for $189.95. Know what those 10,000 "likes" would be worth? Most likely, nuthin'. (Unless you consider it valuable to say "Hey, we got 10,000 'likes.'")

A better question is "How do we get considerably more of the *right* people to follow us on Facebook?"

Of course, it begins with content. Content that resonates – and makes a difference.

What can you do to organically grow your Facebook audience at a faster clip?

Sure, it makes sense to look at content most popular with your competitors' fans. But you're an Optimarketer, right? You're out to produce better marketing than the other guys. So you'll want to dig deep. Brainstorm what you could produce to provide real value. You'll need to devise a posting strategy.

Think about educating, entertaining, and even lifting people up with your posts, in very human ways. If necessary, to nail down an initial hierarchy of exciting content priorities, run a web-based research study.

Experiment with a range of content that's uniquely yours. If appropriate, try everything from content curation to web video to events. The broader the experimentation, the higher the odds of hitting on breakthroughs.

When promoting educational content like an e-book, use an image (visual Facebook posts often perform considerably better than text alone). Write posts that invite feedback. If you run a contest or premium, use a tab to merchandise your offer and solicit information.

Start posting regularly. Yes, even daily if possible. Begin habitually keeping an eye on your Facebook Page Insights, to continuously improve.

And then begin putting the word out. Start with the obvious: Invite the right subset of Facebook friends to "like" your Facebook page. Link your page to your other web properties and email advertising.

If you own a store, make a sign asking customers to "like" you on Facebook, and include the URL (yes, it can be customized). Think about trying special offers for Facebook fans.

Organic circulation will only get you so far; it's a good idea to experiment with Facebook ads. An interesting test: Is it more productive to obtain a Facebook "like" or a lead from one of your website landing pages?

Both have advantages. Appearing regularly in a Facebook member's newsfeed may be very valuable. But a website landing page provides an opportunity for more useful data collection. You could also experiment with data collection using a tab on your Facebook page.

Testing a combination of Facebook ads and sponsored posts makes sense. Sure, you could rely on what other businesses are doing. But their results involve a different set of variables. Your outcomes may be very different.

Remember, when advertising on Facebook, don't try to attract the world. Aim for *quality*. Pursue people who could become customers. And great ones at that.

BLOGGING HUMANIZES YOUR BUSINESS

Cool thing about blogs: A one-person business could have a more important blog than a 1,000-person corporation. But blogging ain't what it used to be.

At one time, bloggers practically had social media to themselves. Early bloggers didn't compete with Facebook, YouTube, Twitter, Pinterest, Google+, or Instagram for viewers.

So with all of today's options, are blogs still worth the investment? Absolutely.

It's a well-known fact: Websites that regularly "refresh" content rank higher on search engines. A blog makes it easy to continually post fresh content.

SEO enthusiasts know blogging is an opportunity to raise search rankings where they matter most, by posting regularly on topics tied to high-priority keywords and phrases.

In blogging, frequency is monumentally important. Many businesses with blogs that draw a large number of the right readers – and leads – post every weekday. Even several times a day.

From a direct response standpoint, blogs are a chance to build a subscriber list, allow readers to profile themselves, and nurture prospects.

All of this is good "blocking and tackling." But is that all there is? Absolutely not.

My friend Eliot Frick, founder of Bigwidesky, talks about the urgent need for businesses to become more human. I suggest you invest 18 minutes in his "Geese from Bottles" TEDx talk. You'll find it on YouTube.

Now back to blogging. Here's the thing: Blogs humanize businesses. Or at least they have that potential.

We all know businesses have a human component; they're about more than a physical product. Your blog enables your employees to build relationships with more prospects and customers than they'd reach via other means.

Of course, a blog is a chance to transfer knowledge, but it could be more than that. Is your business about more than just making money? This is your chance to show it. With your blog, you're able to share what your company stands for: its corporate values and beliefs.

It puts a human face on your business by allowing readers to get to know your people: their opinions, interests, and passions.

But the success of any blog largely depends on whether it provides substantial value to a relevant audience. This can be accomplished in a variety of ways – including the hybrid known as "infotainment."

We operate with a bias toward visual posts, including web video when appropriate. But posting YouTube videos and photos isn't a comprehensive solution. So we like to cover relevant, fascinating, and even entertaining topics that haven't been addressed elsewhere – and invite readers to participate.

You'll find multiple routes to blogging success, but it always requires serious thought. Start by setting objectives. Then survey the current landscape, take stock, and offer something uniquely glorious.

Creating a better mousetrap isn't enough. You don't want to have an excellent blog that very few people read. You need to promote it.

Share your posts across social media. Even write individual emails to bloggers and journalists who may find a post very relevant to their readers. When your blog becomes an exceptional educational resource, think about syndicating it. You'll find plenty of tools online.

Speaking of which, you may have heard of RSS (Really Simple Syndication). RSS feeds allow readers to subscribe to blogs, news sites, and other online destinations, and get all their updated content in one place.

Is RSS still relevant for bloggers? Well, Google discontinued Google Reader due to declining usage. But a new generation of RSS tools like Flipboard and LinkedIn Pulse are creating slick experiences for mobile users. If you're serious about blogging, these exciting tools are worth checking out.

Finally, I want to emphasize that bloggers need to integrate offers and calls to action into their blogs more effectively. Some response-oriented bloggers place a relevant offer and call to action in every post. Maximizing revenue from your blog enables you to raise content quality, so why not turn as many readers as possible into leads – and customers?

GOOGLE GREATNESS

Remember "Video Killed the Radio Star?" If someone were to compose a song about the rise of search engines, they could call it "Google Killed the Yellow Pages."

Let's say a 40-year-old guy living in Secaucus, New Jersey, glances at his foot one day and notices a bunion. Odds are quite low he'll open a print directory, but there's a very high chance he'll Google "podiatrist Secaucus" – or similar terms. The same is true for thousands of other types of consumers and business people.

That, in a nutshell, is why Google's market cap is among the highest on earth. Optimarketers understand not just how to operate Google's cool tools, but also the company's motives.

Google is out to maximize profits, of course. The search giant knows it accomplishes this by giving users consistently excellent experiences.

Without getting into the weeds of Google AdWords, let's run through what it takes to optimize paid advertising on the world's biggest search engine.

On the front end, it's worthwhile to use search engine tools to identify keyword search volume and pricing. Once you understand the size of an opportunity and its cost, you're in a good position to assess whether it could be a winnable option – and what you'll need to succeed.

Google assigns your keywords and phrases a Quality Score based on how relevant it finds your ad to related searches; how relevant searchers find your ad (based on clicks); the experience you give users who click; and other factors. A higher Quality Score gets you higher in Google paid search rankings and a lower cost for each click.

Optimarketing practitioners get higher Google Quality Scores in a variety of ways, including optimized content offers, with ads that merchandise offers extremely well – and attract the right audience.

Optimarketers also run interesting segmentation schemes using ad groups (a set of keywords and ads grouped together – e.g., a building contractor could have separate ad groups for kitchen and bathroom remodeling).

What's more, Optimarketers regularly run tests of major elements: keywords and ad groups; offers; ad copy; landing pages; geography; Google search vs. partner search sites vs. display partner sites; user devices; among others.

Not content to merely track clicks or even form completions, Optimarketers work to get return on marketing investment data from each test.

What does it take for marketers to see *spectacular* Google AdWords outcomes? First, they work the fundamentals very well (e.g., content, copy, keywords, landing pages, testing, and of course, tracking). But they also dig deeper to make unusual connections and uncover profitable keywords off the beaten path; present refreshingly different content that compels viewers to act; conceive directions for search ads that go outside the norm in relevant ways; and use exceptional landing pages that elevate outcomes dramatically.

Optimarketers outmaneuver, outthink, and outwork competitors.

The difference could be a unique emotional appeal in a Google AdWords ad; a remarkable video on the landing page that rocks viewers; a new approach to collecting prospect information; a sudden move in response to a relevant event; or even a decision to test Google remarketing, so people who visit your site also see your ads as they visit other sites on the web.

Optimarketers approach Google AdWords and other search engine marketing options without biases. I once visited a company that had spent more than $90,000 on pay-per-click marketing – because PPC just *felt* more economical. But after they finally got around to looking at net results, they realized they got only a handful of leads routed to sales, and zero conversions.

In some cases, other online sources will be more profitable than Google AdWords – including other search engines. As well as sponsored posts (and ads) in social media, email sponsorships, and cost-per-lead deals that tout your content and vastly expand your reach.

You should approach each option without bias, test when it makes sense, and make decisions based on facts.

Certain options will be considerably more expensive on a per-contact basis, for sensible reasons. AdWords ads on Google search may yield, on average, more motivated prospects than Facebook or LinkedIn advertising – and you'll tend to find that fact reflected in the pricing of each.

But don't think Google searchers are always superior online prospects. They aren't. Another site may enable you to isolate a key demographic (e.g., Vice Presidents of Finance reachable through LinkedIn advertising).

You should expect conversion rates to be different on Google search than on their display network (partner sites not owned by Google but deemed relevant). Marketers use search sites to connect with prospects closer to making a buying decision and the display network to reach prospects earlier in the buying process. Again, that'll be reflected in pricing.

Don't be seduced by attractive front-end math. Sometimes the cheapest cost-per-lead option ultimately proves to be among the most expensive in ROI terms when conversions are counted. Never forget in marketing it's the bottom line – not the initial cost – that ultimately matters.

Your best protection is to test no more than necessary to obtain projectable results and track meticulously to the ROI level.

EXCEPTIONAL WEB VIDEO FOR SOARING ENGAGEMENT RATES

Television is the most compelling communication medium ever. Nothing conveys emotional ideas like TV.

Web video is the power of TV – without the waste. Marketers can confine video content to an audience as small as one person or as large as millions.

Demand for video is skyrocketing: YouTube is now the world's second-largest search engine (after you know what) – and the site gives marketers a variety of promotional options to boost video views and leads.

A recent Pew poll found that 78% of online adults watch or download videos. That statistic will undoubtedly rise in coming years.

Potential uses for video are numerous. Besides YouTube, video may run on your home page to perform important chores (e.g., promote sign-ups); it could be a key component of sales presentations; it may be used in your email marketing to engage a higher share of prospects.

In one split-run test, we saw email advertising with a video offer pull about 600% more clickthroughs than an ad for the same product without a video offer. That change was certainly at the super high end of the spectrum, but it illustrates the potential power of video.

Many marketers with marketing automation use web video because it's easy to consume. Those two-minute videos create meaningful moments with customers and prospects that are tracked in ways that impact lead scoring. When web video is used in email marketing to the database with no form completion required to view content, engagement rates – and leads routed to sales – may soar.

Businesses creating video frequently feature talking heads: company employees running through product or service benefits or giving demos, and customers offering up testimonials. These are all potentially valuable. But there's more to web video. Way more.

Many marketers should augment their basic videos with productions tied to high-impact campaigns. These videos should be designed to make noise, get people talking, and get them to share what they see.

Videos with an extra-special quality will often be scripted – but some of the most interesting options won't require that. Regardless, many will have qualities typically associated with excellent TV commercials – only they won't feel like commercials. They'll be educational.

We've noticed many marketers, particularly in B2B, have difficulty imagining what's possible with video. There's at least one interesting video direction for every marketer. If a marketing team lacks the skill to grow interesting ideas, they should recruit an outside team to make it happen.

Marketers need to think of videos not as one-shots but as opportunities to maintain dialogue. Think series. Imagine producing a set of videos many prospects and customers can't wait to see – that happen to provide essential educational information and help move prospects through the sales process.

One reason many marketers don't even attempt to produce interesting video: fear the budget will be outside the acceptable limit. While it's true that imaginative video often costs more than simple point-and-shoot content, many marketers are able to fit stellar video into their budget.

Don't make the mistake of thinking your video must go viral to be successful. Virality hardly ever happens. And it isn't necessary.

SHOULD WEB BANNERS BE CONCEPTUAL OR OFFER-CENTRIC? YES

Unlike textual search ads, web banners let marketers place conceptual and even animated advertising in front of consumers on relevant websites.

Marketers often wonder if these ads should emphasize a concept or offer. Optimarketers often do both by combining an arresting concept *and* offer in a single awareness-building, response-producing banner ad.

With web banners, you're usually able to include multiple panels, either via Flash or simple gifs. So you could lead with an excellent concept and mention of the outstanding offer on the first panel, and blow out that offer on the second one.

The concept you display in a web banner could grab prospects emotionally – and make a big difference in the measurable outcome. But that doesn't mean banners that lead with a concept always win. It's often best to test a banner that features a concept against one that leads with an offer.

Whatever you do, you'll want to treat your online billboard like a highway one. Remember: Eyeballs are moving fast, so you can't weigh your banner down with too many words. To prevent "banner blindness" (banners ignored by viewers), color and animation may prove valuable.

And what about low banner response rates you've been hearing about? It's true

107

– web banners often pull response rates lower than, say, Google search ads. But when you make a good media buy, that's reflected in the price.

Even the highest-pulling media converts only a miniscule percentage of an audience into leads or orders. At the end of the day, measurable marketing is a mathematical exercise. If a website or network of sites delivers a reasonable share of your audience, and the price is also reasonable, you may want to run a low-cost test to see how the math nets out, and compare banners against other sources.

THE CASE FOR DIRECT MAIL (YEP – POSTAL MAIL)

A client once said she added up the hefty volume of email she received in an average day, realized she often received no postal mail, and concluded it made sense to give direct mail a go.

Direct mail has impressive advantages: It's dimensional, personal, and involving. It carries a higher cost per contact than most media, so you generally can't afford much waste. But it also pulls a higher response rate, on average.

When used in conjunction with other media, such as email or phone, direct mail could be a key contributor to response rates not generally seen when using digital marketing alone.

Targeting possibilities of direct mail tend to eclipse other media. In some cases, direct mail is the *only* way to reach certain prospects.

Here's an example of how precise you can be with direct mail: Let's say you sell enterprise security software. Major financial institutions are a sweet spot. And your field reps need to get before executives responsible for information security. Your list selections could include financial institutions only; an employee size of 5,000+ only; Chief Security Officers, CIOs, and VPs of IT only; and even people responsible for buying security solutions.

In the past, creative professionals outside the measurable marketing field looked down on direct mail. Strange, because it's an outstanding canvas for creativity. As my first boss in direct mail, Neal Friedman, liked to say, "the only limitation is your imagination."

Direct mail production formats have never been more interesting. Of course, your package could be dimensional – a concept in a box. Or it could contain a fun involvement device. And if you have the data for it, printing can go right down to the individual level. Yep, you could have thousands of different versions.

Do letters still work in direct mail? Absolutely. Especially when they're beautifully written. But not in all cases, so it's a good element to test.

While we're on formats, let's put to rest the notion that a cheaper in-the-mail expense is always better. Back to our enterprise security software example. Think a postcard would be the optimal way to get a Chief Security Officer to respond?

Probably not. If it's about profit maximization and not cost minimization, go with a format that takes into account the prospect, product, offer, and concept. (The concept ought to drive the format, not the other way around.)

Will direct mail work for your business? Of course, the only way to know is to (you guessed it) test it.

BROADCAST AND PRINT ARE DECLINING – BUT OPPORTUNITIES ABOUND

On the evening of February 28, 1983, approximately 106 million Americans watched the "M*A*S*H" finale. Fast forward to May 21, 2012 – last episode of another hit series, "House." Fewer than nine million Americans caught that one.

Head over to a newsstand to grab this week's copy of *Newsweek* and you'll notice … it's not there. In 2012, after 80 years, the newsweekly's print edition ceased to exist.

Television, long the undisputed champ of brand advertising, keeps losing eyeballs to digital. Direct marketers know print response rates have been declining for years.

But with crisis comes opportunity. For measurable marketers, television and radio offer substantial targeting – by geography, interest, age, income, and more. With a far lower cost per contact than, say, direct mail, marketers using broadcast media can afford a higher level of waste. And good deals are waiting to be had.

Broadcast media is by no means relevant only to packaged goods advertisers. A local pizzeria may get an inexpensive buy on local cable – and make it pay. The consumer software company may find talk radio a major free trial source. An orthopedic surgeon who invents a new product for people in chronic pain may earn more from a single infomercial than he ever made as a clinician.

Some TV and radio advertisers will run on a "PI" (per inquiry) basis and pay only for results (e.g., leads that arrive via a dedicated toll-free number). Print advertisers will buy remnant space for 50% or more off rate card.

It's by no means all doom and gloom in the traditional media world. This year's Super Bowl drew 111 million viewers. (If more Big Game advertisers integrated the web into their ads in exciting ways designed to secure opt-ins for email, the database marketing possibilities would be amazing. But that's another story.)

Again, measurable marketing is largely a mathematical exercise. Brand-appropriate media properties are available for marketers in a full range of categories, at prices that couldn't be had even a decade ago. It's a good time to get creative – in media planning.

THE NEW
WORD OF MOUTH

Long considered the strongest advertising of all, word-of-mouth has undergone a transformation.

First, let me assure you that traditional word-of-mouth remains alive and well. Parents still take their baby to a photo studio, and when they love the pictures, phone friends to share the experience.

But now they often share in other ways: by posting photos on Facebook (with name of photographer and hyperlink included), tweeting details, or writing a review on Yelp.

Marketers can encourage social sharing ... often by asking. Let's say you're a barber. After finishing a haircut, your customer says "Best haircut I've had in years." Simply ask "Ever go on Yelp?" If he answers "You bet I do," you may want to say "If you wouldn't mind posting what you just told me, that would be awesome." There's a decent chance he'll do it.

But before you launch a strategy for review sites like Yelp, please take seriously what I'm about to say. Never (repeat: never) put words in your customer's mouth and ask them to place your words on Yelp or other review sites. And never, ever pay customers or compensate them in any way for endorsements.

To businesses that are newcomers to social media, review sites are often scary. One question we frequently hear: "What if people say bad things about us?" Yes, some customers will walk out of the barbershop and post a negative comment. But that's okay.

A site like Yelp gives a maximum of five stars to each rated business. If a business has 25 glowing five-star reviews out of 25 reviews, even if they're all true, some readers will think the business owner gamed the system. So some negative reviews raise credibility.

By doing what I've described, and continuously operating in an above-board manner, good businesses have little to worry about on review sites – and a lot of opportunity for new business.

But the new word of mouth is more than social sites. It's "brand ambassadors" chosen to represent a brand on college campuses or elsewhere. It's well-connected "agents" who sign up to try products before the public and share their experiences online and offline with friends and colleagues.

WHERE DOES PUBLIC RELATIONS FIT INTO ALL THIS?

Public relations ain't what it used to be. Yeah, publicists still work closely with journalists; help businesses win awards; arrange speaking slots; and assist in investor relations. But today's outstanding PR people are intimately involved in online media as a means of winning minds and hearts.

You've heard about the great power shift in communications, from businesses to consumers. Today a 78-year-old grandma with an active Facebook account could be a publisher of sorts.

These days, publicists are listening carefully to what consumers are saying online; starting and participating in important conversations; and creating content that influences consumer behavior. They're doing all this in relevant, genuine, timely, brand-appropriate, smart ways.

And like their direct response brethren, they're regularly experimenting and keeping score, to continuously improve.

SMALL SPACE, BIG CHALLENGES

Small ads should be treated differently from large ones. Because size matters (couldn't resist).

In small space, getting to the point immediately is usually the most profitable way to go. Being obscure is never a good idea in marketing, but in small space it's often deadly.

Conceptual work that would typically win in large space can't generally be executed properly in an area the size of a postage stamp.

That said, there's already way too much undifferentiated advertising, and there's never a good reason to run me-too ads anywhere, including small space. So please don't knock off your competitor's headline, body copy, or offer.

One way to stand out is through use of an excellent offer merchandised in the headline and detailed in body copy. Or with a creative approach that attracts precisely the right audience but breaks the mold.

It makes sense to open things up and try something different, because a special advantage of small space – particularly online – is testing ease. In Google AdWords, for as little as a few bucks, you can do split-run testing of different appeals and quickly declare a winner. So when in doubt, test that idea.

LANDING PAGES: THE UNDERESTIMATED WORKHORSE

Landing pages are where digital marketing games are often lost or won. But in many cases they're treated as an afterthought. Let's take a moment to discuss how to optimize them.

Imagine you're responsible for a search marketing program. You're paying an average of $4.40 per click. You've learned that if you merely bring respondents to your home page, fewer than 1% will convert to leads. So you've created a dedicated landing page for your marketing program. Even better, you've decided to test a variety of landing pages and track each separately.

Start with the headline – an element that contributes big time to landing page outcomes. In many cases, a landing page with a strong headline that merchandises an offer will do well. But of course, that's not the only way to go.

When generating leads, on the landing page, you want to give prospects what they need to feel compelled to take that next step. This could be an easy-to-understand definition of your product; a credibility enhancer; answers to key questions; or some combination thereof.

If prospects reach the landing page from advertising containing little information, they may need more details on the page to understand what they're getting into. Nevertheless, a lead generation landing page shouldn't be a novel.

To optimize compliance on lead-generating landing pages, it's a good idea to restate the offer. Really merchandise it. Even mention it one last time on the button near the bottom.

You want to obtain the optimal amount of data from prospects – but the more information you solicit, the lower the percentage who'll complete the form. So ask yourself whether you want more registrations or more data to help you sell.

Think degree of difficulty (known among landing page aficionados as "friction"). The more you require of prospects, put them to work, or confuse them, the lower the percentage who'll submit a completed form. Information management is important: The page should look inviting, attractive, and easy.

Your lead generation form shouldn't be buried. In fact, very often, the lower the form on the page, the lower the odds of getting it filled out. It's best to place the form "above the fold" so it's viewable without scrolling. Your form – and other landing page elements – should work well on a full range of browsers and devices.

Landing pages designed to transact business should be treated differently from lead-generating pages. In these cases, particularly when prospects reach the page after receiving scant information, longer copy will tend to do better. That's why you see landing pages for one-step selling containing hundreds of words or more.

A major way to go beyond the status quo of landing pages designed to transact business is to improve their graphic design. Many look similar. Similarly lacking in credibility. They resemble the salesman you don't feel you can trust. Headlines aren't believable. Clichés abound. Testimonials lack a last name and, as a result, are perceived as fiction. They try readers' patience.

Getting beyond ordinary means regularly experimenting with landing pages. Video, offers, graphic design – all major variables are worth testing.

Usually the majority of website leads come from a small number of landing pages. It's crucial to optimize them.

CONCENTRATION OF FORCE

Marketers have kicked around the term "impact" forever. But how does one really optimize it? Three words: concentration of force. When marketing messages are spaced far apart, they carry less impact than when they're delivered in a concentrated timeframe. This means three touch points spread over a three-week span may be far more effective than over a three-month span. Add to this the impact of a media mix rather than a single medium, and you've got the makings of something extraordinarily successful.

As a test, write an email with the aim of receiving a response. Send it to someone, then phone two weeks later. When you allude to the email, that person may say "I don't remember getting it." But call a day or two after sending the email to another person and he'll be far more likely to recall it.

Concentration of force is powerful.

CASE EXAMPLE: CHRIS BEAUDOIN PHOTOGRAPHY

The most responsive campaign we've ever worked on included three media: "clutter-busting" postal mail, email, and telemarketing. All executed in under a month. It was for Boston photographer Chris Beaudoin, whose clients have included major consumer brands and advertising agencies. Chris has long been known for making photo sessions as stress-free as possible. So to a handpicked list of crème de la crème prospects, we sent a box with a working blood pressure monitor and headline that read "One prop you'll never need when working with Boston photographer Chris

Beaudoin." Result: 51% of recipients took a meeting.

SEGMENTATION SUCCESS

It's obvious to most marketers that generalized messages rarely work. People prefer specificity: marketing that appeals to their narrow interests. You're reading a book on marketing optimization. If you wanted an affiliate marketing book, you would have bought one instead.

The practice of segmentation – slicing an audience into a narrow group and appealing specifically to their interests – nearly always improves the response rate over generalized messages. Yes, you can almost bank on some lift from a segmentation scheme. So the decision to run one is always a no-brainer, right?

Not really. First, you must be able to isolate and market to that segment at a cost-effective rate. The potential value of treating that segment differently must exceed the added cost by an appropriate margin.

Opportunities for segmentation have never been more intriguing. Marketers can now go beyond traditional schemes (e.g., demographic) and segment based on actual behavior.

Segmenting by persona – a fictional character representing a particular type of prospect – is an excellent way to grab prospects emotionally. Personas also enable you to focus on prospects with the characteristics of your very best customers and create content aimed squarely at them. So you attract more prospects who resemble customers you covet most. But as with all segmentation schemes, it's important to test before you leap.

Technology has created spectacular possibilities in segmentation. With variable data printing (VDP), you can segment by individual. Yes, one-to-one marketing really, truly has arrived. And it's more economical than many marketers believe.

Smarter segmentation cuts wasteful marketing and creates more satisfying experiences for customers – and marketers.

LEAD GENERATION: WHAT YOU'RE REALLY SELLING

Many lead generation practitioners who've been at it for years aren't aware of this invaluable maxim: In lead generation, you're not really selling a product or service but an offer – an opportunity for prospects to take the next step.

Look at it this way: If your business product sets customers back $125,000, virtually no rational soul on earth will read your email ad and press an "Order" button. In this case, if you present what you consider sufficient information to secure a purchase – while burying an educational offer – you'll most likely shoot yourself in the foot. By concealing that easy-to-act-upon offer, you'll suppress the response rate. In this type of situation, it's usually more profitable to prominently merchandise that no-commitment offer.

Another way to slash response: Say too much. Prospects won't agree to learn more if they believe they already have everything they need to know. Don't make them feel sated. Shorter copy tends to be optimal in lead generation.

It's also a good idea to hold something back – and I'm not just referring to information. We've developed extremely successful marketing programs with two-part offers: When a prospect raises her hand, so to speak, she gets Part A of the offer, and if she qualifies and takes a conference call or in-person meeting, she gets Part B (the latter may be seen as considerably more valuable).

What also works: content tailored for prospects in different phases of the so-called "marketing funnel." The funnel metaphor is based on a related acronym that's good to remember: A.I.D.A. (attention, interest, desire, action). Used by marketers forever, it takes a variety of forms. Recently, some marketers have been switching from funnel to life cycle, with the customer at the center.

But let's return to the still-popular funnel metaphor: Prospects at the top of the funnel may be ripe for entertainment; those closer to converting into customer-hood may be ready for a far more product-centric (but interesting) appeal, like a feature-rich demo.

As for lead generation offers, they certainly don't have to be educational. Hell, these offers don't necessarily require any connection to the product or service ultimately being sold.

Your lead generation offer is nothing more than a means to an end. Anything that enables you to add the right prospects to the database, move them downstream in the sales process, and get conversions at the optimal rate will do the trick.

More than ever, "softer" (lower commitment) offers make the most sense – largely because they may add 25% or even 250% more leads to the database than "harder" (higher commitment) offers. In most cases, virtually all leads that would have landed in the database from a harder offer will also come in from a softer offer.

Yes, softer offers tend to create more "false positives." But they often bring in more prospects that could convert over time. Thanks to email marketing and its ability to cost-effectively keep you in touch with database prospects and allow them to profile themselves, it makes sense to err on the side of a larger rather than smaller marketing database. Especially considering how fast many database records decline in value.

Frequency is a hugely important contributor to conversion rates; most prospects simply aren't ready to convert the first time they hear from you. Having the chance to nurture these leads may enable you to convert a far higher share over time.

Augmenting the database with useful data for lead scoring (e.g., company size) is quite easy. This is important, because all leads aren't created equal. Once you know what various types of leads are worth, you're in the best position to know how much to spend to convert them. A minority percentage of leads should receive far more spending than most because of their high potential contribution to profits.

Every lead generation veteran knows it's fairly easy to fill the database with suspects – or worse, utterly worthless records. You generally get back what you put in. Media, creative, offer – they all contribute enormously to the quality of leads that land in your database.

But remember, the game will often come down to the so-called reply device: the card or landing page that summarizes the offer and solicits feedback from the prospect. The more friction-free you make it, the higher the percentage of prospects who'll comply.

That said, we have clients with small sales organizations that want to operate at the high end of the lead quality spectrum because of resource constraints. In some cases, we've asked respondents to answer a mini questionnaire, to identify a subset of hot prospects and categorize leads. But again, if you're out to hear from as many prospects as possible, the more hurdles you put up, the fewer prospects you'll hear from.

CASE EXAMPLE: UNICA

Unica (now part of IBM) makes marketing automation software. Realizing that marketing executives who didn't embrace this new technology were clinging to marketing from a bygone era and risking career obsolescence, we decided to play off this psychology in a humorous way. Our agency developed an integrated campaign consisting of dimensional mail, email marketing, and telemarketing. The "clutter-busting" mailer included a box designed with seventies-style art and the headline "A return to Funkytown for enlightened marketers." Inside the box sat a disco mirror ball with the headline "These have come back. Marketing techniques from that era haven't." Body copy informed prospects that if they met with a Unica sales rep, they'd get a motor to spin that disco ball "and start your own disco inferno." Result: 9.1% of campaign recipients took a meeting in some form with Unica. The campaign won second-place honors at the New England Direct Marketing Association Awards for Creative Excellence.

ONE-STEP SELLING: THE TOUGHER MARKETING JOB

Early in my career, nearly 100% of my work involved one-step selling: marketing that went for an order as the next step. People have asked if lead generation is harder than one-stop selling. My standard reply: "Are you @!#$%^& kidding?"

Lead generation is definitely easier than one-step selling. In the former, you're generally requesting relatively little of the prospect; in the latter, you're asking for an order on the spot.

When the prospect is a stranger and the product is unknown, how does a marketer bring someone all the way to the sale? David Ogilvy said the answer was long copy. Was he right?

Yes, he was. Long copy often suppresses response rates in lead generation, but often wins in one-step selling. We've run controlled tests of short versus long copy in one-stop selling and seen a marked lift via the latter. You can certainly run your own tests and see for yourself.

In one-step selling, prospects need enough information to make the buying decision. Certainly, brand reputation enters into the equation. If I receive advertising inviting me to order a Cadillac online, General Motors will probably do better with the right longer copy presentation. However, because I've been exposed to Cadillac advertising my entire life and respect the brand, I'll need less information than if I knew nothing about the carmaker.

In all cases, it's not enough to nail basics like the concept, art direction, and benefits. You've got to put yourself in the buyer's seat (pun intended). This means anticipating objections. In the case of the Cadillac buyer, many prospects will be price-resistant. So the cost needs to be justified. And it's one thing to ask people to write a big fat check on the spot and another to offer more comfortable terms. Carmakers are masters at making expensive pieces of hardware seem affordable and even economical.

Besides overcoming objections, key questions must be answered, including "What do current owners think of the car?" Of course, many prospects will simply view ratings online from third-party sources. But testimonials from actual customers will help.

In advertising copy, benefits indeed sell more than features. But there's also a place for features – under those benefits. In our Cadillac example, buyers need details. Lots of details – on safety equipment. Time from 0–60 MPH. The GPS system. Accident avoidance system. Audio speakers. And a lot more.

CASE EXAMPLE: MICROFRIDGE

One of the best entrepreneurs and sales pros I've worked with is Bob Bennett, founder of MicroFridge. As a young engineer, Bob developed the first combined refrigerator, freezer, and microwave oven. It ran on a single cord and drew fewer amps than a hairdryer. This at a time when college students were using hot plates to cook food in dorm rooms with primitive electrical systems. MicroFridge put an end to that fire hazard. When we began marketing MicroFridge to colleges that approved them for dorm use, we asked to send mail not using the MicroFridge logo but instead each college's own letterhead. Presentations were personalized, benefits-oriented, fact-based, and comprehensive.

Very often, choice is deadly in direct marketing, but in this case, given the nature of the product and audience, we concluded it would be best to let students choose between leasing and buying. Result: The order rate went above 20% in some schools, and MicroFridge changed college dining forever.

GOOD AND NOT-SO-GOOD PARTNERSHIPS

Optimarketers find the most efficient ways to acquire customers. Sometimes a single relationship translates into hundreds or even thousands of customers.

Of course, partnerships take a variety of forms. In marketing, they often involve a deal between two complementary firms, to create synergy. For example, technology firms often partner with marketing services firms. Marketing services firms gain access to prospects, offer a more complete solution, and get a commission each time they refer a customer. Technology companies gain referrals from marketing services firms, provide a value-added service to customers, and raise customers' odds of success with their products. Win-win, as they say.

Statistically, most partnerships don't pay out. But those that do often more than compensate for failures. In many cases, 20% or fewer of partnerships account for 80% or more of partner revenue. It clearly pays to focus on those with the best payoff.

In the "performance marketing" realm, we find another type of partnership: the affiliate program. As an affiliate, you're paid for each visitor, lead, trial, or customer that results from your efforts. For example, if you've built up a database from your marketing, and email an invitation to buy a product from an information publisher, and the publisher pays you for each customer who buys, you're an affiliate.

In some affiliate programs offering educational content, publishers pay as much as 100% commission. These are usually cases where most or all of a publisher's revenue comes from other, more lucrative sales from readers.

There's a dark side to the affiliate game: product "reviewers" who aren't really offering legitimate reviews but merely trying to attract customers. Along with other advertisements containing false and misleading claims.

In partnerships (and your other marketing) do the right thing – from an ethical and bottom-line standpoint.

"DO WE HAVE A REASONABLE SHOT AT SUCCESS?"

The answer to that is often hugely helpful when contemplating whether to pull the trigger on a new marketing program. If, for example, you need a double-digit response rate to merely break even, you'll probably want to put money into something else. Here's a simple but worthwhile algebraic formula:

Sales(x) = Variable Expense(x) + Fixed Cost + Required Profit

Let's say an item sells for $100 and costs you $30. Your fixed costs are $5,000. You want to know your breakeven point, so you list the required profit as $0. The equation would look like this:

$100x = $30x + $5,000 + $0

So the final calculations would be:

70x = $5,000
x = 71.43 orders to break even

Now simply ask "Is it reasonable to achieve that order volume?" We call this the "reasonability test."

This is an easy way to avoid entering into no-win marketing situations. In some cases, after running the numbers, you'll find that by adjusting the variables, you'll turn a situation that initially looked bleak into one with reasonable odds of operating in the black.

Managers often ask what the "average" response rate is for a particular type of marketing program, across all marketers on earth. There's really no such statistic. A variety of variables contribute to outcomes. Each case is different. For example, you may have an above-average conversion rate and thus require a below-average gross response rate. Better to focus on your unique requirements.

And on a related note ...

SUCCESS COULD BECOME ALMOST MATHEMATICALLY INEVITABLE

Really. A profitable business with a good product and evolved sales team will probably run a profitable marketing program if they simply nail the basics, including testing to arrive at the optimal marketing mix.

In business-to-business and some business-to-consumer marketing, revenue in year one of a relationship is so high on average, one conversion makes an entire marketing program profitable.

That's why it's a mistake for decision-makers to get scared off by marketing programs with a relatively high cost-per-contact. If a prospect is worth considerably more, it only makes sense to spend considerably more to turn that prospect into a customer. All customers are indeed not created equal.

Marketers with a small budget often pull the plug on pay-per-click programs before running adequate tests. A marketer who sells a service with a $4,500 average gross margin per customer may become scared after obtaining 300 Facebook clicks and no customers. But in reality, to do well, the business may need only one customer for every 900 clicks.

Optimarketers *calmly* test in projectable ways to obtain high odds of success on rollouts. With a large enough sample size on an initial test, you could operate at more than 95% confidence with a 10% limit of error. This translates into 95% odds your rollout will be within 10% of your test result. How often in business do you get odds that good?

MANIPULATE THE BIG ELEMENTS

Optimarketers don't tinker at the margins. They work the big elements. Because (it's worth repeating) insignificant changes tend to result in insignificant change.

Classic example I like from the world of direct mail: I once saw a business test the style of its bulk mail indicia. I could easily think of 50 tests that would go ahead of that one.

Focus on major changes in the creative message, offer, media, follow-up, and other big aspects. To make a serious difference, run tests that are different.

LESSON FROM
THE MAGAZINE
PUBLISHING MODEL

Fascinating question marketers in magazine publishing like to kick around: When does it make financial sense for a renewal series to end?

Answer: When it becomes cheaper to acquire a new customer than go for the renewal. Think about it.

MINIMIZING MARKETING EXPENSES IS OVERRATED

No Chief Marketing Officer ever went before a Board of Directors and said "The marketing campaign bombed, but we cut costs by 10%."

Have you ever needed a piece of clothing, bought the cheapest one you could find, and ended up having to quickly replace it with a more expensive alternative? When that happened, you paid considerably more than you would have, had you made the best purchase initially. This is a common occurrence in marketing.

In marketing, in business, and in life, higher quality almost always costs less.

When you watch a high-end TV commercial and think about the money that must've been spent producing it, remember: The media expense may ultimately run in the tens of millions. Therefore, the difference between a low- and high-end production may be an almost immaterial contributor to total cost. In fact, it may be financially irresponsible to go cheap on production. In a case like this, it's a marketer's responsibility to protect that vast level of media spending.

Every professional marketer eventually sees the term "cost-effective" treated as a synonym for "inexpensive." Actually, if that low-cost alternative bombs, it may be the most expensive option of all.

Marketers also quickly learn that there are few second chances in this business. Very often, you have only one shot. Therefore, you want to do everything possible to make it succeed.

When running a test, you don't want to do it in such a slipshod way that after it's completed, you're left wondering if the outcome would have been different had you conducted a proper test.

Spend what's needed to do the job right the first time, and you'll have more successful outcomes ... the first time.

A CAVEAT ON SHORTCUTS

I'm going to save you a huge amount of time by sharing a simple truth: Not many shortcuts exist for marketers. Optimarketers tend to work considerably harder than ordinary marketers.

You'll find no shortage of products telling you how to use marketing to quickly and easily make a fortune. In about 100% of cases those opportunities are a mirage. They don't work. For anyone.

You certainly don't have to always outwork your competition. But you'll probably have to outthink them.

DATA.
WHO EVER THOUGHT IT
WOULD BECOME COOL?

As a young marketer, I was taught that everything begins with the marketing database. To this day, when I speak with marketers about their challenges, I ask database-related questions at or near the beginning of our conversation.

In marketing, most profits tend to come from the marketing database. It may be a gross understatement to call it fundamentally important.

Response-oriented marketers are taught that great database marketers regularly solicit and receive feedback from prospects and customers to improve marketing and sales. They become adept at getting people to profile themselves.

With tools like marketing automation, marketers no longer have to solicit as much feedback as in the past. They can progressively acquire valuable information from known visitors over time, to improve sales and marketing. Thanks to rich data easily available from outside sources, what's solicited from prospects today is often cut-to-the-chase information of substantial value.

Reminder on marketing automation: If you're in B2B marketing and don't currently have a system, get one. And if you already have one, take advantage of important features like triggered email programs, a dashboard view of marketing campaigns, and lead scoring. You're even able to reach an agreement with sales on what constitutes a sales-worthy lead, and end a long-running conflict between marketing and sales.

While you're at it, if you haven't begun using a customer relationship management (CRM) platform, get one of those too. Among other things, it'll make your marketing database far more valuable. The ROI from marketing automation and CRM should be outstanding.

In database marketing, the more useful the data you collect, the more opportunities you have to optimize monetization of your database through more relevant targeting. Many if not most marketers don't collect enough feedback for the database from customers and prospects. Yes, there are trade-offs in feedback solicitation, but good incentives and experimentation will help you identify the optimal amount of information to solicit.

Augmenting your internal database with data from external sources opens a variety of opportunities, including predictive analysis. So you find more prospects who resemble your best customers; make previously unproductive portions of the database productive; and eliminate previously wasteful marketing.

What about "big data," you ask? Is it everything it's hyped up to be? Big data alone isn't much to get excited about. Many businesses are drowning in it. It comes down to what one does with it.

Consider the reality of converting prospects. A large number of variables may impact a sale. And of course, some variables are far more important than others. If you're able to take advantage of internal and external data sources in ways that make sales and marketing more efficient and effective – while producing an excellent return on investment – you're leveraging big data in exciting ways.

I'll share an example from a fascinating business our marketing agency has worked with: Lattice. They help companies with lots of data (and customers) run marketing and sales more efficiently. Lattice goes beyond typical lead scoring and works with what they say is "every relevant buying signal in the world" – thousands of attributes. One example among many: When a business announces expansion plans or a layoff, Lattice takes that into account in its automated recommendations.

So sales reps get leads more likely to close and even receive insights for more relevant talking points. To prove its value, Lattice encourages split-run tests of a prospect's current approach against the recommended Lattice approach. In head-to-head tests, Lattice doesn't tend to lose.

Optimal use of data often makes a major difference, so don't think of "big data" as just another meaningless buzzword. It isn't. And don't sit on the sidelines and observe while competitors take advantage of new data tools, merely because you feel this ain't your thing. Companies helping marketers make the most of their data are good at helping client-side executives who aren't data wonks.

And don't make the mistake of believing that excellent use of data will be a cure-all. Reaching the right audience at the ideal time with a boring, uninspired, trite creative appeal is, to say the least, unfortunate. You never want to snatch defeat from the jaws of victory.

Remember: Optimarketing is about optimizing *all* major marketing elements.

A BRIEF ANALYSIS OF ANALYTICS

Many marketers receive a shitload of analytic data. If we plotted the data deluge on a bell curve, in the middle we'd see a vast area representing moderately useful information. At one end we'd find a relatively small area representing virtually or even utterly useless information – and on the other an area of comparable size for extremely useful information.

Naturally, it's best to focus on the extremely useful end.

Optimarketers concentrate on what matters in bottom-line terms. They care about moderately useful analytics (e.g., page views, opens, clicks) – because they're capable of improving profits. But they're after the marketer's Holy Grail: return on investment data, with a lifetime value calculation. Because marketers can't fully know how much to spend to acquire a customer until they know what one is ultimately worth.

Some companies run up $15,000 in marketing program expenses to acquire an average customer – because each on average is ultimately worth $375,000. (By the way: That's a 25-to-1 ratio of revenue to marketing program spending.) That same business may triple marketing program expense to acquire one particular type of customer … who happens on average to be worth six times the norm – or $2.25 million. When you reach this level of knowledge, you're in the ideal position to optimize marketing spending.

With lifetime customer value in hand, you can calculate your ultimate return on marketing investment – by source. Even by individual test cell. When a

144

marketer realizes he's been spending 15% of his marketing programs budget on three websites pulling in 2% of measurable revenue from marketing, and 6% of the budget on two sites that account for 19% of revenue, he obviously knows where to shift spending.

Sure beats counting impressions (the number of times an ad is displayed) and obsessing over results information of little or no consequence.

A caveat from friend and über direct marketer Jaffer Ali: Because marketing is changing at a faster-than-ever clip, old lifetime value data could be misleading.

But when you've reached the ultimate level of results analysis and understand your true return on marketing investment (using data that remains relevant), you're able to justify full funding of your marketing program to anyone. Including the most hardened skeptics (more on that shortly).

Are excellent analytics expensive? Not necessarily. Google Analytics is incredibly insightful – and free for most users. A marketing automation platform, on the other hand, may cost a fair amount per month – but its ROI could be outstanding.

Analyze what counts, but don't try to analyze everything. You'll never succeed. As Einstein noted "Not everything that can be counted counts, and not everything that counts can be counted."

JUSTIFYING MARKETING TO ANYONE, INCLUDING SKEPTICS

Every now and then we run into them: "anti-marketers" – executives, often with a chip on their shoulder, who don't believe in marketing. Amazingly, a few even work for companies selling products and services for marketers.

These people claim marketing is a waste of money. I've reminded a few of them if they were right, billions or even trillions of dollars had been wasted over more than a century on marketing worldwide.

Imagine for a moment anti-marketers were in fact correct, and marketing funds essentially amount to money down the drain. They could be eligible for a Nobel Prize in economics. Think of the financial savings.

But we all know great brands never would have put all that money toward marketing over all those years if it never made financial sense. Skeptics who think marketing is unnecessary generally have little or no marketing skills. Some compete with marketing for budget dollars.

When facing hardened skeptics, the best way to get your marketing program funded is to make a bulletproof financial case: another reason to run projectable tests that minimize initial financial exposure and maximize potential payoff.

Ever notice that sales groups usually don't have the funding difficulty we often see in marketing? That's because a Sales VP, via track record, can demonstrate that $1 in fully funded expense for a new sales rep will tend to yield, say, $12 in revenue. Chief Financial Officers relate to (you guessed it) financial data.

When you can prove each dollar will ultimately return $10, $25, or $50, you're far more likely to get funding you need. And when those same executives see how revenue associated with rollouts far exceeds the cost of losing tests, they're far more likely to embrace aggressive marketing tests.

SWEAT THE DETAILS

Top marketers and other professionals sweat the small stuff. Steve Jobs didn't just obsess over things like a graphical user interface; he aimed for his computers to be beautiful on the *inside* – in places virtually no user would ever see.

First-rate copywriters may go through (no kidding) 25 drafts before the client ever sees the deck. And great marketing managers check, re-check, and check again for errors and flaws.

Granted, you don't want to go overboard and let the pursuit of perfection interfere with your need to regularly execute. But it's a good idea to expend serious energy on the details.

CHOOSING YOUR IDEAL MARKETING AGENCY

I've run a marketing agency for a quarter-century. For a variety of reasons, including the obvious one, I thought it would be good to address this topic.

Excellent marketing agencies contribute enormously to the success of businesses. In some cases, they transform company value.

When choosing an agency, start by thinking carefully about what you need and want. You'll save everyone time.

Be respectful of each agency's time. I recommend you not ask for what's known as "spec" (free) creative work, media recommendations, or marketing plans.

It may be tempting to get all sorts of marketing services for free, but it's easy for these exercises to become counterproductive. For one thing, spec campaigns are generally created without access to complete information and with a variation on an agency's usual process. So a spec campaign that runs may be half-baked – or worse.

Many agencies refuse to do spec work – so by requesting it, you may eliminate the agency most likely to help you succeed. A more effective way of knowing what an agency can do for you is to study where they've been and what they've accomplished. Most important of all, look at their work. Without excessively taking advantage of their expertise, engage them in lengthy discussions on marketing. Understand how they think. Get to know them. Make sure the chemistry works.

Whatever you do, don't reject an agency that asks very challenging questions. The best ones are interviewing you to see whether there's potential for a great relationship, including great outcomes.

And don't make the mistake of believing the ideal agency has worked with an almost identical client. That's often a recipe for standard work. Diverse experience with a wide range of clients is a major part of what agencies bring to the table.

By understanding a marketing agency's accomplishments, work, services, methodology, and fees – as well as by speaking with relevant clients – you'll get everything you need to make an informed decision. And you'll set the stage for a productive working relationship.

SELLING MARKETING "SOLUTIONS"

When I opened my marketing agency, I had no experience in sales. None. But I had a passion for solving marketing problems. So I simply contacted businesses I thought we could help and offered to get together and talk about their marketing challenges.

It worked. I soon learned that prospects didn't want to be pitched. I later realized a large number of sales reps were attending seminars on "solution selling": events designed to teach reps to sell "solutions" rather than products.

You'll do better by selling solutions. But you need to be able to deliver the goods. Learn more than your competitors about marketing in your niche. Become what's known as a "trusted advisor." Liberally share what you know. Not only is this approach more profitable, it's also more fulfilling.

OPTIMARKETERS EVOLVE. QUICKLY

Ted Leonsis famously said "digitize or die." At the time it seemed a little harsh. But boy, was he right. Marketers either evolve or die. And those who evolve at an ideal pace … well, you never know what'll happen.

A great example from the entertainment world, of course, is The Beatles, who first appeared on the Ed Sullivan Show in 1964 and broke up in 1970.

Think about how rapidly their music evolved over that six-year span. America initially fell in love with songs like "I Want to Hold Your Hand." But by their last studio album, "Let It Be," their music had changed dramatically.

Like The Beatles, Optimarketers continually evolve. They're never considered an oldies act. They keep breaking new ground by building on success. By running wildly varying experiments. By staying up-to-date. And by never being satisfied with the status quo.

Optimarketers relish risk-taking. To borrow from a saying on our agency's most popular t-shirt, "Playing it safe is risky business."

OPTIMIZING THE CUSTOMER JOURNEY

"Customer journey" may seem hackneyed, but it's an important term that describes the interactions a customer has over the life of a relationship.

Earlier generations of marketers mostly focused on customer acquisition. "Lifetime value" (LTV) was covered in marketing books, but few businesses were able to really optimize it. Today, thanks largely to affordable technology, marketers are able to optimize every major phase of the customer journey.

Optimarketers start off in a stronger place by engaging a higher share of the right prospects at a highly cost-effective rate. They don't just convert customers; they convert a better class of customer. After efficiently turning prospects into customers, they make the most of retention, upsell, cross-sell, and referrals.

Yep – Optimarketers sweat all of it.

Every major customer segment has its own funnel or life cycle, with relevant messages, content, and other appeals. Each conversion automatically launches the next activity. (Another reason why marketing automation is so important.)

Think of the relevant offers you receive when you buy on Amazon. They're based on your history and relevant customer behavior. Via constant tracking, the model gets more and more profitable. And of course, Amazon serves recommendations dynamically.

Obviously, no marketer can address every potentially worthwhile activity. So

Optimarketers focus on the most profitable customer segments that emerge from research, testing, analysis, and hard work.

BUILDING A
"MARKETING MACHINE"

Sophisticated marketers crave scalability, consistency, and projectability (as well as other things ending in "y").

Among other statistics, some have memorized their average response rate, percentage considered sales opportunities, rate of converting opportunities into customers, and average revenue per customer – by source.

Through trial and error, marketers are even building reverse marketing funnels. They start at the bottom of the funnel, with the revenue goal from marketing. From there, they run the math on required conversions, opportunities, and raw leads at the top of the funnel. Optimarketers have it down to a science.

We need more marketers like that.

Marketing can be a consistent machine. But operating it requires skill. And it needs plenty of upkeep.

Like farmers, the Optimarketer's work is never done. The marketing machine requires a steady stream of high-quality content optimized to produce the desired level of exposure, leads, and sales. We may be an industry that relies on autorespond, but great marketing programs don't run on autopilot. They need to be managed. Constantly.

In marketing, nothing remains the same. Profitability of customer sources may eventually erode. Some sources will disappear entirely. Another reason it's key to aggressively and regularly test major elements.

I don't want to run the machine metaphor into the ground, but it's important to remember that Optimarketers fire on all pistons. For the machine to really hum, experimentation, conceptualization, content, media, technology, team-work – it all should be optimized.

WHAT IF YOU WORK IN A SUBPAR MARKETING ORGANIZATION?

I've worked for and with great, good, and not-so-good marketing organizations, and learned valuable lessons from them all.

This shouldn't come as a surprise: You'll tend to learn the most useful stuff from great and good organizations. For one thing, the best marketing groups are embracing the best techniques.

It's sad to see marketers with a lot of potential remain, for years, in a place mired in mediocrity – or worse.

Of course, it isn't always easy to exit a bad situation. Extricating oneself from the wrong position becomes increasingly difficult as a worker ages. People acquire mortgages. Have kids. Life gets more expensive.

I've seen great people do exceptional work in not-great organizations. But in most cases, marketers aren't going to do great work in a not-great place. So the answer is to do the best work you can where you currently are, while looking for something better. If you're living from week to week and need the job, you probably don't want to put your paycheck at risk.

It makes sense to keep smiling. Be a happy warrior. Build as much justification as possible for an excellent marketing organization to bring you on board. Then, when you get the chance to jump ship, take it.

THE "HOME RUN GAP"

More than a decade ago, a client uttered a particularly revealing – but quite disappointing – comment.

"You guys want to hit home runs. We just want singles."

Rarely are marketers that candid about a willingness to accept ordinary work.

No question about it: Aiming for excellence is harder. It does indeed take more work. More courage. Even more integrity. That's why it's uncommon.

In the marketing field we see far too many singles hitters. Reasons why include lack of budget and time as well as organizational and cultural challenges. Indeed, the biggest barriers to success are often internal rather than external. But the greats find a way to jump over any and all hurdles.

The "home run gap" (lack of marketers who swing for the fences) creates an opportunity for those who consistently aim to hit it out of the park.

MARKETING IS A TEAM SPORT

Some marketers try to be the equivalent of a Swiss Army knife. They act as marketing manager, creative director, art director, webmaster, video producer, marketing automation administrator, and more. Very often, they're pressured to do as much as they can on their own to reduce short-term costs. In many cases, this ends up being more costly in the long run.

In "Magnum Force," Clint Eastwood said "A man's got to know his limitations." While it's true that marketers often must wear a variety of hats, it's important to be keenly aware of what's outside your zone. If you're outcome-oriented, you never want to be a mile wide and an inch deep.

A quote attributed to Confucius is worth mentioning: "To know that you know what you know, and that you do not know what you do not know, that is true wisdom." Optimarketers know what they don't know and bring in those in the know. They don't operate with major voids that could compromise outcomes.

Marketing is more complex than ever. Optimarketers don't do as much as possible on their own. It's about choosing the most *profitable* (not necessarily the cheapest) options.

So budget permitting, Optimarketers regularly weigh value vs. cost of working with internal and external specialists. Whenever possible, they don't do the heavy lifting – including formulating strategy – alone. They put the right resources together to optimize outcomes.

We're interdependent. Marketers who know we're all in this together achieve at the apex.

HIRING OPTIMARKETERS

My brilliant aunt Jenny (Rosenthal) Piekny, who exited Nazi Germany in 1939 and lived to age 100, liked talking business with me. She particularly enjoyed hearing about different characters our agency encountered. When I explained how some people behaved – good and bad – she would say something worth remembering.

"It's his (or her) nature."

Aunt Jenny believed people could acquire many skills, but character traits (e.g., generous vs. selfish, honest vs. dishonest, sensitive vs. coldhearted) generally couldn't be taught.

Optimarketers hire people who bring to the job the right basic equipment – including education, training, and experience – plus something more.

Traits worthy of respect.

Over the years, I've increasingly asked myself "Do I admire this candidate? Would I enjoy working with her?" I'm not talking about people who share my passion for genealogy, non-fiction reading, or the New York Knicks. I don't care about that.

As leader of an Optimarketing team, you need to attract excellent people. With hearts in the right place. Ready to pull out all the stops.

So let's dive into what really matters when it comes to creating that optimal fit. Like so much of Optimarketing, it isn't mysterious.

161

For starters, a simple truth: People most likely to accomplish extraordinary things have done so in the past. I'm referring not only to marketing. The young person who launched a social enterprise at age 17 and raised $2,600 for a worthy cause certainly has the makings of an Optimarketer.

But in marketing we also have late bloomers. Some were slackers through sophomore year of college, took Marketing 101, found their calling, and were on their way. Others entered marketing from a very different career later on and did incredible work.

The interview is your chance to understand the candidate – how smart, resourceful, enthusiastic, genuine, and hardworking they are. To see whether or not they share your values. And of course, learn if the chemistry is right.

Something important to glean at this stage: How assiduously a potential employee acquires new tips, techniques, and skills. Optimarketers are lifelong learners.

Unless you're out to discover how an applicant responds to absurdities, interviews shouldn't be about off-the-wall, trick questions. Asking "What do you consider your biggest weakness" has got to be one of the most pointless questions of all.

We like finding out about big accomplishments, challenges overcome, hidden talents, and how a person thinks. In one case, two applicants were both excellent candidates. So I wrote a marketing quiz that included issues, problems, and opportunities they'd potentially face on the job. One emerged as the clear winner, and became an invaluable colleague.

A former boss, Bob Russell, said he always tried hiring people smarter than he. You want people with complementary skills. Colleagues who'll challenge you. You don't want a collection of sycophants. (On a related note, you always want to be on guard for applicants out to simply tell you what they think you want to hear.)

Something else you don't need: a bunch of coworkers who sorta seem the same.

Like healthy families, healthy businesses are diverse. It's best to mix skills, strengths, genders, ages, races, backgrounds, and more. Remember, diversity is a key contributor to marketing innovation.

Periodically, candidates emerge out of the blue who don't fit an open slot – or any job description you've ever posted. But they've done their homework and make an excellent case for your creating a position. Whenever possible, businesses should seize these opportunities.

You need to hire people not only for where you are but also where you want to be. Much of your ability to recruit and retain people who build your business will come down to the marketing organization you run.

A recent Randstad study found that flexibility, corporate culture, and rewarding high performance were key to cultivating productive and happy employees.

Happy employees are indeed better for your bottom line. Another recent study, by UK economists, found that happy employees are on average 12% more productive.

My not-surprising observations: Collaborators and nurturers, rather than command-and-control types, attract and keep better people. Businesses that maintain a healthy work/life balance are the most appealing. And entrepreneurial organizations are magnets for Optimarketers – the best marketers of all.

DEFEATING THE GREAT ENEMY: PROCRASTINATION

I've known marketers who talked … and talked … for years about developing great marketing but never actually did it. Low budget, fast timetable, wrong environment – they always found an excuse.

A popular problem is "chicken and egg." The marketer says he can't run extraordinary marketing until business picks up. But of course, sales are depressed because marketing is ordinary.

Sometimes money simply isn't available to do anything beyond ordinary, and that's all she wrote. But very often, marketers are able to move money around and give excellent marketing a go.

Optimarketers find a way. They aim for greatness. Not next time. This time.

I said earlier the biggest barriers to success are often internal rather than external. Sometimes it's largely a matter of getting beyond your own fears – and yes, excuses.

Some marketers act as if their career will be 3,000 years long. None of us have all the time in the world. So get on it.

"THINK"

That was IBM's motto for many years. It's one idea marketers should steal. I wish I had – early in my career. Here's why.

Shortly after I finished college, a friend approached me with a film he'd produced for nonprofits. He asked me to help him promote it (remember, I had been a marketing major and worked my way through school in marketing, so I was already somewhat experienced). The movie had a beautiful and important message; I was excited to help him market it.

One problem: The nonprofits he targeted had very little money. Many were struggling. It was a "blood-from-turnip" situation. We knew it going in – but chose to overlook that fact. (In retrospect, I was greener than I cared to admit at the time.) Needless to say, the effort was a complete flop.

Very often, answers to big questions are readily available – if you give them just a little thought. Will prospects find that message believable? Is that survey too long? Does that promotion have a reasonable chance of success?

Think about it. Don't just agree with the boss or that close associate. Or succumb to groupthink. Be the clear-headed one. You'll avoid tests that should never run and marketing programs destined to be dead on arrival.

ANSWERING MUCH-DEBATED MARKETING QUESTIONS

Some marketing questions have been kicked around for decades. I'll take a stab at answering a few of my favorites.

Are positive approaches more responsive than negative approaches?

That belief was quite common earlier in my career. I know a good number of marketing executives who refused to run concepts they considered negative. Many still feel this way.

Problem/solution approaches are often productive in marketing. Prospects instantly relate. Of course, when you start with a problem, very often the most productive way to highlight it is to lead with a negative.

We also know emotional concepts often resonate best. In many cases the ideal way to convey them is via a negative lead.

That said, consider Martin Luther King's "I Have A Dream." It's fair to say it was a positive speech overall. It didn't simply resonate – it changed history and helped earn the civil rights icon a national holiday. As well as a monument on the National Mall.

In certain cases, positive is more responsive than negative. But some of our bigger successes have included concepts that led with a negative. It's a mistake to rule out negative options. Testing a positive vs. negative lead may be a good idea.

Is a "straightforward" creative approach best?

In meetings, you may sometimes hear executives suggest going with a "straight-forward" creative approach – or something like that.

Marketers who haven't worked with interesting concepts sometimes operate with this bias. You don't generally see it among marketers who've run campaigns containing excellent concepts.

You'll also notice marketers with this bias tend to advocate undifferentiated creative work. Why would anyone think me-too advertising would pull better?

Optimarketers understand the mechanics of responsive marketing. They don't embrace unclear, obscure creative approaches. Nor do they think hitting prospects between the eyes, beating them over the head, or spoon-feeding them is *ipso facto* optimal.

All things considered, what customers and prospects take away is far more important than how a presentation begins.

Is "interruption marketing" dead?

Nope. So-called interruption marketing isn't close to extinction. But it has undoubtedly lost its pre-eminence and much of its power.

Media we rely on for entertainment – including TV, radio, and even Facebook – is delivered at no charge to consumers. Interruption marketing is a key part of the deal.

Optimarketers don't just run superior concepts in these media; they also look for interesting ways to engage with prospects beyond the initial ad – and to grow the database for more cost-effective marketing via email, SMS, and other means.

Businesses already producing an acceptable return on marketing investment from such media should by no means abandon it for no rational reason. Nor should they deliberately annoy, disrespect, or do something unethical.

Are shorter headlines always best?

In a word, no. David Ogilvy joked that he made it into the Advertising Hall of Fame largely on the strength of an 18-word headline ("At 60 miles an hour the loudest noise in this new Rolls Royce comes from the electric clock"). Don't run with a flat headline strictly to be as concise as possible. Don't withhold the flavoring. Don't cut into bone. But do make your headline no longer than necessary – all things considered.

Is marketing mostly an art or a science?

That's an easy one: Optimarketers see it as both. Marketers who care far more about one than the other tend not to fire on all pistons.

When the price rises does demand ever rise as well?

I've been involved in thousands of marketing tests. In controlled price testing, I've never seen a price increase result in increased demand.

Marketers have repeatedly said "We raised the price and it didn't affect order volume." Whenever I've asked for details, they either weren't available, or when they were, we learned the test wasn't controlled or it was blown.

Your economics professor was right about price elasticity: When all other factors are held constant, if you raise the price, expect a reduction in orders. But in net terms, a price increase is at times more profitable.

Is the media rep right when he says increased frequency will dramatically change our response rate?

Probably not. When advertising doesn't have a pulse out of the gate, it doesn't tend to acquire one through increased repetition. A dog generally remains a dog. However, it's quite common for a response rate to increase with added frequency.

THE MIND OF THE OPTIMARKETER

Philosopher and baseball great Yogi Berra allegedly said "Baseball is 90% mental and the other half is physical." The same is essentially true of Optimarketing.

Ordinary marketing is formulaic. Follow a set of "proven step-by-step techniques" and learn to operate some tools, and you too can achieve perfectly average outcomes.

Marketing optimizers think, talk, and act differently. Optimarketers:

- Don't delegate leadership or play follow the leader. They blaze new trails and make unpopular decisions when necessary.

- Aren't satisfied with the ordinary and repel mediocrity. They take steps necessary to make innovation happen.

- Don't just swing for the fences; they aim to drive it out of the park and into the adjacent neighborhood. Optimarketers sometimes even attempt to hit a home run for the ages. They tune out the little voice that whispers "You can't do that."

- Never scapegoat when failure occurs and know success is generally its byproduct.

- Aren't egocentric. They put outcomes ahead of selfish interests. Optimarketers eagerly share good results. And credit.

- Are genuine. They don't play games or operate with hidden agendas. Optimarketers don't needlessly put people to work. They consistently mean what they say.

- Focus on outcomes. They're not out simply to please the boss or an internal client or friends in advertising. Optimarketers play it for those who really matter: customers. They care far more about producing powerful marketing than PowerPoint presentations. Optimarketers concentrate on elements that matter.

- Maintain an entrepreneurial spirit, even inside mega corporations.

- Are perennial students. They never stop learning through experimentation and other means. Optimarketers are the antithesis of the know-it-all who doesn't know it all. They love surrounding themselves with people capable of teaching them stuff. Optimarketers are lifelong students of the craft.

- Choose collaboration over command and control. They encourage opposing views. In a meeting, when an Optimarketer is the highest paid person in the room, it's often hard for an observer to tell.

- Don't just outthink competitors, they outwork them. Optimarketers have an outstanding work ethic. They avoid counterproductive shortcuts.

- Love their work. Marketing isn't just an occupation, it's also a passion.

- Are in a hurry to produce spectacular work. Optimarketers operate with the fierce urgency of now.

- Don't simply give instructions: They provide them in ways that optimize odds of realizing the best outcome.

- Treat everyone – from the CEO to the assistant's assistant – with respect.

They believe treating people well isn't just the decent thing to do; it's also good for business.

- Know how to find, motivate, and keep great people. They recognize that marketing is a team sport.

- Don't bury their head in the sand. When a strategy bombs, they don't stand around with hands in pockets. They change the strategy. When it's time to have a difficult conversation, Optimarketers do it – sooner, not later.

- Have the courage of their convictions. They don't sell out. When necessary, Optimarketers speak out.

- Don't rely on gimmicks.

- Are self-aware. They know their limitations – and shortcomings. Optimarketers plug important gaps. They defer to experts.

- Believe there's something to Malcolm Gladwell's rule that mastery takes 10,000 hours (or 5,000 if they've studied Steven Kotler's *The Rise of Superman: Decoding the Science of Ultimate Human Performance*). They put in the required time and effort to rise to the top.

- Are analytical, but don't fall victim to analysis-paralysis. They execute. Constantly.

- Choose positive over negative reinforcement. They create a positive work environment for everyone.

- Run factual marketing. They tell the truth.

- Challenge the status quo. They're naturally rebellious.

- Don't engage in marketing filibusters. They run great marketing rather than merely talk about it.

- Are generous – and reasonable. They expect people to be paid fairly for their contribution.

- Don't let insecurity keep them from making the right moves. Colleagues with strengths or skills they lack don't intimidate them. They welcome the addition of players with a variety of gifts.

- Are obsessively focused on quality but don't allow the pursuit of perfection to create stagnation.

- Know that cost minimization isn't a goal, and the most cost-effective alternative may not be the least costly one upfront.

- Admit their mistakes. They promptly correct and learn by them. They don't make excuses.

- Don't delude themselves into thinking their marketing is virtually perfect when it isn't.

- Deliver high service levels, but don't behave in subservient ways.

- Are agreeable, even when they disagree. They know agreeable people generally accomplish more.

- Treat outside resources as partners, not vendors.

- Are loyal.

- Care more about what gets done than how it gets done.

- Are flexible. They rarely consider anything "carved in stone."

- Create solutions, not problems.

MARKETING IS A NOBLE PURSUIT

In polls, marketing professionals have been rated lower than lawyers, bankers, and politicians – but higher than car salesmen.

Our field doesn't exactly have a stellar reputation.

I don't blame the public. Many marketing practitioners regularly stretch the truth or make things up. Most fabricators aren't even good at it: Their work lacks verisimilitude, the appearance of truth.

But lots of marketers refuse to be involved in marketing that isn't legitimate. Marketers doing the right thing have every right to take pride in their work.

OPTIMARKETERS CHANGE THE WORLD

Marketing optimizers are capable of great things. For starters, we introduce people to better ways of living – and working.

When marketers successfully launch new businesses, we often contribute to raising the employment rate. Among my proudest accomplishments: businesses we've helped that have employed thousands of people with good-paying jobs.

But of course, Optimarketers don't just help businesses. They elect officials who enact important laws. And raise money for worthwhile causes.

You have a chance to rock the world. Optimize the time you have.

CLASSIC MARKETING BOOKS THAT CHANGED MY CAREER TRAJECTORY

"I have seen one (ad) actually sell, not twice as much, not three times as much, but 19 ½ times as much goods as another." – Tested Advertising Methods

Bill Bernbach's Book – Bob Levenson

Confessions of an Advertising Man – David Ogilvy

Crossing the Chasm – Geoffrey Moore

Direct Mail Copy That Sells – Herschell Gordon Lewis

Direct Marketing: Strategy, Planning, Execution – Edward Nash

Hey Whipple, Squeeze This – Luke Sullivan

Ogilvy on Advertising – David Ogilvy

Permission Marketing – Seth Godin

Positioning: The Battle for Your Mind – Al Ries and Jack Trout

Reality in Advertising – Rosser Reeves

Scientific Advertising – Claude Hopkins

Successful Direct Marketing Methods – Bob Stone

Tested Advertising Methods – John Caples

The Practice of Creativity – George Prince

What's the Big Idea? – George Lois

CONNECT WITH ROBERT ROSENTHAL

Author/speaker website: http://robertjrosenthal.com
Contenteurs agency website: http://contenteurs.com
Optimarketer blog: http://optimarketer.com
Optimarketing LinkedIn group: http://optimarketing.net
Contenteurs Facebook page: http://facebook.com/contenteurs
LinkedIn page: http://linkedin.com/in/robertrosenthal
Twitter: http://twitter.com/robertrosenthal
http://twitter.com/contenteurs